AF477997

Cinema – Italy

Cinema – Italy

Stefania Parigi

Translated with a Preface by Sam Rohdie
Edited by Sam Rohdie and Des O'Rawe

Manchester University Press

Manchester and New York

distributed in the United States exclusively by Palgrave

Published by Manchester University Press
Oxford Road, Manchester M13 9NR, UK
and Room 400, 175 Fifth Avenue, New York, NY 10010, USA
www.manchesteruniversitypress.co.uk

Distributed exclusively in the USA by
Palgrave Macmillan, 175 Fifth Avenue, New York,
NY 10010, USA

Distributed exclusively in Canada by
UBC Press, University of British Columbia, 2029 West Mall,
Vancouver, BC, Canada V6T 1Z2

British Library Cataloguing-in-Publication Data
A catalogue record for this book is available from the British Library

Library of Congress Cataloging-in-Publication Data applied for
ISBN 0 7190 7860 6 *hardback*

First published 2009

18 17 16 15 14 13 12 11 10 09   10 9 8 7 6 5 4 3 2 1

The publisher has no responsibility for the persistence or accuracy of URLs for any external or third-party internet websites referred to in this book, and does not guarantee that any content on such websites is, or will remain, accurate or appropriate.

Typeset in Scala and Scala Sans display by
Koinonia, Manchester
Printed in Great Britain
by CPI Antony Rowe, Chippenham, Wiltshire

Contents

In memory of Lino Micciché, my teacher
not only in my scholarly work but also in my life.

List of illustrations

Acknowledgements

I am indebted to Sam Rohdie. The idea for this book was his, as was the choice of essays. I am deeply grateful for the care and attention he gave to their translation and editing. I want to thank Des O'Rawe for his editorial help and Matthew Frost at Manchester University Press for his patience.

Preface

By Sam Rohdie

For the most part writing on the cinema of Italy, particularly in English, has placed greater emphasis on 'Italy' than on 'cinema'. Some of this writing has been of a cultural studies kind and some have emphasized various, historical and political aspects. In either case, Italian films have tended to become examples or illustrations of something else, and that something else is often Italy. An unfortunate consequence of this is that such writing tends to stress the content and meanings of Italian films more than how they work and are structured.

This collection of essays is important because of its concentration on the structure and forms of the films it discusses. The categories with which it deals – language, light, rewriting, settings, space, time, locations, repetition, mirroring, sound – bring the films into a relation with other films and thereby with the cinema, not only its history, but its possibilities.

The characteristics shared by these essays include a sensitivity and knowledge of the cinema (not only Italian), genuine scholarship, and the ability to see in every detail of the films discussed aesthetic resonances, and indeed cultural ones, to painting, literature, poetry, music. No discussion, I think, of the films of Visconti, Rossellini, Pasolini can ever be the same again after reading this book, nor will the standardized discussions of Italian neorealism endure the ideas brought forward in the essay on Zavattini, which literally opens your eyes and if nothing else re-illuminates the French cinema and the writings and ideas of André Bazin. In this way the familiar (neorealism, Bazin, the *Nouvelle Vague*) is refreshed, made anew and relevant, not simply part of a dutiful historical necessity.

It is not that issues of history, culture and ideology are ignored but rather are enlightened by being seen in their specific and particular operation in the films, that is, how these aspects are made aesthetic as exemplified in the materiality of film. By so doing the films are literally revived, become not only open and exciting, but truly contemporary. They take off, not away from the issues of culture but rather with them, culture made into art. The films circulate in the realm of cinema by creating associations on the basis of form, rather than say, chronology, nationality or politics. And thus in renewing these films and suggesting relations by concentrating, for example on light or sound, the whole of the cinema and its history are renewed.

Introduction

The journeys described in this book were taken during the past fifteen years but refer to a period still more distant. They are journeys in time and of memory about a country that no longer exists: the Italy of Roberto Rossellini's *Paisà*, torn by war and sometimes in conflict with the American 'liberators', a confrontation of cultures, as real now as it was then; the Italy of Luchino Visconti, a territory more cultural than physical, subject to transfigurations wrought by a sophisticated intellectual who viewed the world through the lens of his sensibilities. The paths of this itinerary also intersect with the Italy of Pier Paolo Pasolini in the guise of an imagined ancient world irreparably destroyed by industrialization and consumerism.

In undertaking such journeys, I have embraced the point of view of an historian intent on reconstructing a map that also includes gaps and discontinuities. I have not been tempted to write a tourist guide with familiar and consecrated monuments and landmarks. Had I done so, I would have been obliged to refer to Michelangelo Antonioni's Italy and to the existential unease of the second half of the twentieth century that he documents and also to Federico Fellini's baroque, cartoon-like, provincial lunatic world, so emblematic of a country which has disappeared, yet seems to await its resurrection as new and postmodern.

Had I wanted to travel in that direction I would have included Bernardo Bertolucci, the most international of Italian directors, and also Marco Bellocchio, Italy's most visionary film-maker, who has reflected in his work the upheavals of Italian history and culture.

These journeys are not accidental nor do they lack design. They have an inner coherence in the analyses they provoke and set in train. With the exception of the first essay on Cesare Zavattini, which are theoretical analyses, while the others are films analyses. The historical rather than historiographical dimension emerges through the interpretations of the films and of their relation to other works, realms and meanings. The analyses at times have a strong philological bent, of great assistance in the pursuit of values concealed in the visual and sound structures of the films. I have drawn both from literary and cinematographic material, as evident, for example, in Visconti's experiments in *La terra trema* with the language of Giovanni's Verga's novel *I Malavoglia*, and also evident in the radically elliptical editing of *Paisà*.

The first three essays focus on discussions and films relating to neorealism. They seek problems and inconsistencies in points of view and prejudices that have become institutionalized in popular accounts of neorealism, for example, those linked to the idea of a realism as a mimetic and objective reproduction of reality and those emphasizing a moral stance incapable of developing into an aesthetic one. I have strictly pursued a symbolic dimension beneath the 'realistic' surface of the images in order to be guided by the compositional structure of shots and the rhythm of their associations. I have worked on the echoes of images, released inside and outside the film, and on the rhetorical and stylistic aspects that contribute to the sense of a work, often fleeting and always inexhaustible.

The fourth and fifth essays are dedicated to Visconti's commemorative and antiquarian vein, to the central importance of *mise en scène* (in the theatrical sense) in his films, while the sixth is an attempt to recover an archetypical image in Pasolini's work (the union/contrast between heaven and earth) as revealed in innumerable drafts and rewritings. I have embraced the idea of such reworking and of masquerade, also analysed in the seventh essay (dedicated to Pasolini's *Trilogia di vita* and to *Salò*), as keys to understanding his films.

While leafing through these essays, I have come to realize that they are all traversed by recurrent themes and obsessions: the contrast between – and circularity of – darkness and light, night and day. Darkness recalls the Unconscious, while light is the sign of knowledge, and just as night is inhabited by instincts and dreams, day represents the prosaic rites of daily life and of history. In *Paisà*, a non-linear idea of history makes the arrival of light, usually linked to reason and civilization, coincide with the arrival of death. His characters suffer the Freudian 'discontent of civilization' and die, or more often kill themselves, as gestures of impotence and rebellion *vis-à-vis* history. The conflict between nature and civilization is present in Visconti's world too. In *Il Gattopardo*, history is a spectacle of the compulsion to repeat the past, the vulgarizing by the *nouveau riche* and their killing of beauty in nature and in art.

The representation of primordial elements can also be considered to be derivations of the contrast between history and nature: images of earth, water and sky intermittently mark the dialogue and the images from the credit titles onwards and assume the importance of almost cosmological figures. Pasolini's sky is a place towards which beings made of soil and air direct their gaze in search of the mystery of their origins and of their destiny – 'resplendent nothingness' full of 'tormenting marvellous beauty'. Water, in *Paisà*, is clouded by the dramas of the story (the American 'liberators', the corpses of the partisans), and contains, in the final shot of the film, whirlpools which recall the indifference of nature before individual and group tragedies.

The contrast between darkness and light in *Paisà* and in Visconti's *Vaghe stelle dell'Orsa*... is most incisive and dramatic.

It returns us to the material of which cinema is made, the creations of appearances by light, the fruit of the darkness of a movie theatre pierced by a stream of light projected onto an empty rectangle made of iridescent shadows, reflections, memories and dreams, the dark and light through which we glimpse external and internal worlds, transformed and interpreted, if not from a window, then certainly from a privileged vantage point. The light that lacerates obscurities is a metaphor for knowledge, but also of its dazzle and secret transits. It is light that creates the *figment* of an image, a figment in the Latin sense of *fingere*, that is, modelling, forging, lending shape to shapeless, invisible things, giving colour to the opaque and brightness to the obscure.

1 Cesare Zavattini: neorealism

Cesare Zavattini is principally remembered as a theoretician of neorealism and as the author of the screenplays of some of the major post-war films of Vittorio De Sica (*Sciuscià/ Shoeshine* 1946, *Ladri di biciclette/Bicycle Thief* 1948, *Miracolo a Milano/Miracle in Milan* 1951, *Umberto D.* 1952). In fact, his experience was more extensive and varied. He worked in different media and was especially sensitive to the changes wrought by the spread of new technologies in their impact on traditional forms.

Zavattini was born in 1902, in Luzzara, in the province of Reggio Emilia. He worked as a journalist on *La Gazzetta di Parma* in the 1920s, moving to Milan in the early 1930s, where he worked for the publishers Rizzoli and Mondadori in their popular, mass-circulation publications. He also worked in cartoons and radio. In 1931, Valentino Bompiani published Zavattini's first 'anti-novel', *Parliamo tanto di me,* written in the form of an interior monologue. Zavattini immediately demonstrated his ability to bring into his journalism the fruits of experiments in his other writings, mixing together high- and low-brow thereby upsetting traditional aesthetic hierarchies. Beginning in 1934, he wrote his first screenplays and theorized a new idea of cinema as an alternative to the comic-sentimental film genre (the so-called *telefoni bianchi*) popular during fascism by combining aspects of avant-garde cinema (Dziga Vertov, René Clair) with American slapstick (Charlie Chaplin and Buster Keaton). Zavattini wanted to bring together documentary and fictional fantasy while contesting Hollywood formulas of verisimilitude. He rejected the conventions of linear narrative in favour of a free narration of discontinuous fragments and he was against naturalistic acting and the star system. He displaced these with the everyday and the ordinary.

Zavattini left Milan in 1940 for Rome, where he continued to work until his death in 1989. His ties with the film world expanded. He became one of the most important figures in the post-war Italian cinema. He radicalized his ideas of film as already expressed in the 1930s by emphasizing a moral and political-social commitment.

There is considerable continuity and coherence to Zavattini's thought, beginning in the 1950s, when he took an interest in television, and in the 1960s with his engagement with avant-garde films and films of protest. Zavattini's concept of realism was often reductively interpreted by critics and others as an artistic form tied to the reproductive and mimetic capabilities of film. To the contrary, Zavattini stressed the potential of film to transfigure reality. He never excluded the dimension of the imaginary, always indicating an inter-relation between external and internal worlds as a dominant characteristic of film. He considered the image in terms of its power to bring understanding by an encounter of objectivity and subjectivity. He saw film as a privileged means to experiment with the simultaneity of perception and thought and as an instrument to embark on a philosophical enquiry into temporality and space.

Dreams of knowledge

In an important article, 'I sogni migliori' ('The Best Dreams'), published in the journal *Cinema* in April 1940, Zavattini fore-shadowed, as in a preparatory sketch, the dense network of ideas that he would interweave after the war. 'Nine-tenths of world cinema', he wrote, 'relies on the romantic and the extreme'. Against the uniformity and conventionality of such spectacles, he invoked the sight of a blind man able to go beyond the standardized while nourishing instead fresh forms of creativity. What he proposed were new modes of narration and a focus on things that traditionally were not thought worthy of representation. 'The blind', he provocatively declared, 'are capable of appreciating events considerably more profound than those dear to international scriptwriters; only such events would permit and contribute to a genuine and real revolution: *a film about a man sleeping, a film about a man arguing, without being edited and, I dare add, without a subject* ... An episode which is accidental and without a centre ... The ability to return to man himself as "total spectacle". What a great conquest it would be to contemplate our fellow-creatures in their elementary acts obtained simply by placing the camera on a street, in a room, watching with insatiable patience, educating ourselves.' In short, he argued, the eye must disrupt the usual processes to which today's cinema has trained it and discover not only new ways of seeing but of foreseeing. The eye was to be considered an 'estranged' eye, in Shklovsky's sense, rather than one that reproduced appearances, an organ that did not reflect reality, but instead illuminated and revealed it, as Zavattini would later repeatedly emphasize. Far from constructing abstractions, this way of seeing, by the fact of being rooted in the concreteness of things, of having been caught 'in the earthy truth of their appearance', produced dreams made of the material reality of things, as well-defined as 'the veins on leaves'.[1]

The sense of surprise and wonder – key words destined to reappear in Zavattini's post-war writings – was no longer entrusted to the story-telling and technical capabilities of the cinema, but flowed from a relation of discovery and recognition between the subject who regards and the object regarded. The eyes of the blind open onto a world 'never before seen',

1 Cesare Zavattini, 'I sogni migliori', *Neorealismo ecc.*, ed., Mino Argentieri, Milan: Bompiani, 1979, 39–40.

a pre-grammatical one, the result of a fusion of vision and representation. The 'sogni migliori' ('best dreams') in the title of the article are, above all, dreams of new instruments and itineraries of knowledge.

The experience of the war marked a point of no return for Zavattini. The lives of the people seemed to have been destroyed even to the shape of their ideas and culture. Books of the past resembled a pile of papers gnawed by mice. Writers seemed alone and disoriented, groping with old words, worn-out names and descriptions no longer in contact with real things, 'like fallen crumbs'.[2]

The *tabula rasa* produced by the war required artists to assume a 'terrible inheritance', finding themselves with a historical mission for a revolution in social, aesthetic and existential structures.[3] Changing the forms of art entailed changing the shape of the world, and vice versa. Film, as a mass medium, was called upon to assume that responsibility more than were the other arts. The responsibility was civil and moral. From 1948, it would be called neorealism.

Crisis and research

Neorealism for Zavattini was, above all, a path of experiment and research consequent upon a crisis, essentially one for Italian intellectuals who were detached from the experience of ordinary Italians and in search of new revolutionary links between society and culture, art and life. The territory in which Zavattini moved was filled with doubts and utopian ideals. 'At last,' he wrote in 1946, 'after undisturbed certainties, we are now so unsure that even the most extravagant requests seem legitimate. We are setting sail on the raft of Doubt as if it were the ship of Sinbad.' He went on to say, 'We are creatures frightened by over-confident voices and words since we continue to call things by names that no longer

---

2 The expression appears in various publications after the war, for example in Zavattini's 'I pesci rossi e il disonesto [1946]', in *Neorealismo ecc.*, 55.

3 Zavattini, *Neorealismo ecc.*, 56.

relate to them.'[4]

The culture of doubt was one of direct immersion by the artist into the chaos of facts and of actuality. The horizon was phenomenological. It was close to the ideas of Jean-Paul Sartre and to the reflections of André Bazin and Amédée Ayfre on the cinema. Zavattini provides an existential and philosophical gloss to the artistic act in the form of a continual interrogation of immediate reality, an uninterrupted relation with the other and an experiment in thinking without preconceptions, that is, a thinking shaped and reshaped by direct contact with things and the world.

Such an act of discovery was charged with unreserved emotion executed in the form of a visceral statement of love for the world. This is the point from which Zavattini's evangelical and utopian inspiration arises, but also its non-transcendental nature and physical concreteness. There is a strong Dionysian presence of the exaltation of matter and of vital humours in his thought. Knowledge coincides with experience and gives rise to physical, even sexual, contact with things. Thought is set off through the body, breathing, leaping and at rest.

Film as mass media seemed to Zavattini to be the most appropriate instrument for achieving such direct physical 'exploration', for grasping the fire of facts and flesh. In 1977, recalling his post-war positions, he declared: 'First it was literature that allowed me to dance in the masters's harems, later the instrument was the [film] camera so that, not accidentally, I began to wonder if a scientific device could really be connected with absolute truths, and lend a hand with types of knowledge that could only come from them.' Film, for Zavattini, was an art of presence, while literature, which interposes the mediation of words between author and reality, for him was an art of absence. The instruments of the cinema seemed to reduce to a minimum the distance between words and acts, a position that became increasingly problematic and later would lead him to devise experimental

---

4 Zavattini, *Neorealismo ecc.*, 55.

anti-literary forms as in *Non libro più disco* (1970).

In a striking analogy with the theories elaborated by Pasolini in the 1960s, Zavattini's enthusiasm for the capacities of cinema was accompanied by a feeling of profound dissatisfaction with the means offered by literature. The theory of film becomes, for both artists, a discourse where they can express a passionate love for real life, something more than an occasion for a philosophical discussion of existence. And we can see in their work, significantly, the use of religious terminology that can be interpreted as a necessary corollary to a theory of knowledge based on the sacred nature of physical presence.

When Zavattini says that the film camera leads to the revelation of real life, he does not intend to suggest a miraculous force, but rather its maieutic capacity for activating the process of understanding. It is understanding and not the means to it that is endowed with something miraculous, in that it produces, through concrete experience, self-discovery and the discovery of the other, instead of as an abstraction or a principle before the fact.

Zavattini's epistemological horizon was not very different from that of Bazin, who used the terms 'revelation', 'ambiguity' and 'the mystery of reality' to indicate the possibility of achieving an understanding leading to open rather than pre-established results, in which the gesture of the question counted more than the uncertainty of a reply. It was not by chance that Bazin managed to grasp, better than anyone else, the sense of physical astonishment released for Zavattini in every new encounter. 'The words "wondrous" and "astonishment"', Zavattini noted in 1977, 'are intended to be the price of declaring that what we encounter is more important than what we are accustomed to believe in and assert; we are still too insufficiently astonished by reality: one does not really know reality unless it provokes amazement! It is that wondrousness which, in turn, provokes deeper knowledge'.[5]

5 Zavattini, *Zavattini parla di Zavattini*, ed. Silvana Cirillo, Milan: Lerici, 1980, 93–95.

Open forms

For Zavattini, a dual emancipation of the means of cinema was necessary, namely a break from established industrial structures and canons of representation, in order for it to accomplish its philosophical function to promote knowledge. Already in 1940, among 'the best dreams' was the dream of making the instruments of film available to everyone, 'like paper, ink, plasticine, paint' and 'to introduce film stock and lenses into homes as one might sewing machines'.[6] The director's act of expression, for Zavattini, was the equivalent to that of a writer, as film is equivalent to a book. Several years before Alexandre Astruc's manifesto on the *caméra-stylo*, Zavattini declared that the film camera must be used with the same sense of freedom, variety, subjectivity and independence as a pen and that a director is like a writer facing a blank page or a painter an empty canvas.[7] The deciding factor of the fate of the cinema as commodity was its high cost of production compared to the other arts. 'When film stock becomes cheap, and everyone can own a movie camera, film will become a free and flexible means of expression like any other.'[8] The lightweight camera, for Zavattini, was indispensable for a democratization of the means and methods of production and representation in accord with a dream by Dziga Vertov in the 1920s and that digitalization is achieving today.

Only if free from the constraints of the market, according to Zavattini, could there be film-books with a variety of unconventional lengths (from one minute to twenty-four hours), diverse forms and genres (not only novels, but also short stories, poems, essays, diaries, letters, journalistic reports and investigations) and non-institutionalized modes of exhibition (other than the classic film theatre). For Zavat-

6 Zavattini, *Neorealismo ecc.*, 38.

7 Alexandre Astruc, 'The Birth of a New Avant-Garde: La Caméra-Stylo', *The New Wave: Critical Landmarks*, ed. Peter Graham, New York: Doubleday, 1968, 17–23.

8 Zavattini, 'Alcune idee sul cinema', *Neorealismo ecc.*, 106.

tini, it was the industry that determined the tyranny of the plot, which, for him, was the initial obstacle to the ability of film to discover things, in that the plot substitutes hierarchical formulas of story for an open, unplanned relation between the film camera and the world. Hence, instead of investigating existence phenomenologically, it reduces it to an anecdote, to a closed progression of stereotyped events performed by character-puppets rather than by real human beings.

The classic rules of narration and representation seemed to Zavattini to be 'codifications of limitations', artificially interposed screens between the individual and reality.[9] Neorealism, which he considered to be a permanent awareness of the means of cinema rather than the expression of a transitory historical moment, implied a firm refusal of any grammar and instead the adoption of open forms to be experimented with according to circumstances. The 'will to know', he wrote, 'invents its own method and risk and experiments, in an interpretative sense, with objects, persons or situations with which, as a *conditio sine qua non*, it has finally decided to establish a relation'.[10]

Zavattini's aversion to standard structures extended to contesting the actual organization of making films. Performing a somersault and throwing off his own profession as scriptwriter as one might a priestly cowl, he declared that the figure of the scriptwriter should be abolished, insofar as the film director has no need to assume the role of a theatrical *metteur en scène*, but rather must immerse himself in the adventure of discovery, developing things as they 'go along', unconstrained by a script.

In tune with Rossellini's post-war cinema and anticipating the *nouvelles vagues* of the 1960s, Zavattini celebrated the supremacy of filming over plot and the immediacy of an unprogrammatic encounter between artist and materials. He contrasted the layered and flexible structures of diaries, of

9 Zavattini, *Neorealismo ecc.*, 105.
10 Zavattini, 'Neorealismo, fatto morale', *Neorealismo ecc.*, 149.

subjective, autobiographical journeys truly experienced, to the closed artificial structures of novels. 'When I speak of a "diary" or say "everything as if it were a diary", I am issuing an invitation exactly to that, to the narration of life not in obedience to a plot, but to actual existence.'[11] For him, the experience of real life should substitute itself for the experience of the story. The director, for Zavattini, must throw himself into the world and establish contact with people in flesh and blood instead of with fictitious characters contrived by narrative conventions.

The idea of a text perennially *in fieri* (in the making), capable of following the disordered flow of events without cause and effect, is present in Zavattini's work in his earliest literary efforts, in which he rejected the presence of a third-person narrator. This writing was anti-novelistic. The 'sogni migliori' ('best dreams') of the 1940s were that kind of anti-novelistic dream at odds with the position taken by the *Cinema* group of Mario Alicata, Giuseppe De Santis and Luchino Visconti, whose model for a renewal of Italian cinema in a realistic direction was the nineteenth-century novel, Giovanni Verga pre-eminently. Singularly, this oscillation between weak and strong narration was destined to resurface after the war. Most of the Marxist critics grouped around Guido Aristarco and the journal *Cinema Nuovo*, well into the early 1950s, promoted the revival of the nineteenth-century novel as a counter to the dispersive force of Zavattini's writings and of the practices of the most advanced neorealist films, which they accused of simply recording news stories and describing current events, without a critical perspective or articulated political position. The theories of György Lukács and Andrei Zhdanov were contrasted to Zavattini's enthusiasm for experiment that tended to become more radical, renouncing the concept of the unified work and replacing it with the idea of a field of research, a true virtual laboratory that opened the way to new structures of television investigation, *cinéma vérité* and *direct cinema*. Zavattini worked on bringing together documentary

---

11 Zavattini, 'Alcune idee sul cinema', *Neorealismo ecc.*, 103.

and fiction, direct testimony and reconstruction, the essay and the narrative, and inscribing within these a continuous self-reflection. His formal position was a necessary condition for what might be called *pathos morale*, the consideration of style as a social and political practice, thus shattering their separation in traditional aesthetics.

His thoughts on a diary film, journey film and inquest film began in the early 1950s. It set in train the most lustrous phase of Zavattini's ideas, bringing to the foreground his desire to make cinema a space of activity for artist, poet and anthropologist rather than for the novelistic narrator. He was committed to re-establish a modern 'science of man' by means of new ways of seeing, feeling and thinking that would be profoundly different from those that were institutionalized.

The time of experience

The 'bias' of equality, as Zavattini figuratively defined it, was the basis for a new sense of temporality. Abandoning the novelistic in favour of the diary entailed the coexistence of all moments in an individual's life, without imposing a hierarchy dictated by rules of narrative that require the rejection of material not directly narratively functional. In contrast to the temporality associated with the heroes of classical spectacle, Zavattini preferred the shapeless, unmotivated flow of daily life.

From the early 1940s, he suggested that the cinema be used as a microscope of time, capable of decomposing the dynamics of a body in movement into infinitesimal parts. The idea of distending a minute of real action into ninety minutes of film time, by 'accelerating, slowing, reversing, restarting, stopping, expanding, decreasing, pairing, separating, putting one in front of another and behind another', belonged to that period.[12] The anti-naturalist concept of time evident in edit-

12 Zavattini, 'Un minuto (1940–1943)', Straparole, Milan: Bompiani, 1967, 10.

ing procedures of the avant-garde was the basis of Zavattini's project, at once similar to it and different, namely to show 'ninety consecutive minutes in the life of a man' to whom nothing particularly significant happens.[13] In both the avant-garde *and* in Zavattini's project, the temporal element is freed from an aesthetic of verisimilitude and naturalist illusion, replaced by the material concreteness of time.

From this experimental and radical opposition to the linearity of the novel, Zavattini wove a dense network of close and distant fraternal relations: the idea sketched by Fernand Léger in the 1920s to make 'a film of "24 hours" in the ordinary life of an ordinary couple' and the *mostrum* created by Andy Warhol in 1963 with *Sleep*. But on an ethical as well as aesthetic grounds, he shared most with the phenomenology of Bazin and his ontological realism. The idea of a cinema with a duration opposed to that of classical editing is linked for Zavattini and Bazin to a desire to be caught up in the seamlessness of existence in order to grasp the experience of it before grasping its sense, or more precisely to grasp its sense through the experience. 'There is a thrust towards becoming interested in others', Zavattini declared, 'no longer in accord with the synthesizing narratives of the past, but rather by analysis leading to a recognition of the existence and pain of people living in real time'.

His analytical attitude is based on a relational and empirical idea of knowledge, devoid of idealism. It implies an interpenetration between subject and object existing in the same temporality. Zavattini saw the cinema as the most congenial means for investigating and revealing this simultaneity of the individual and of others at their most critical moments. He invoked, as if it were a new theological virtue, the 'patience' of a continual gaze that never interrupts contact with physical reality, nor detaches itself from things in order to represent them. Together with 'patience', which was his favourite term, he employed others such as 'remaining on the scene,' 'a cinema of encounter', 'a cinema of presence', 'a cinema of

---

13 A recurring formulation in Zavattini's writings of the period.

cohabitation', all of which point to the need of the 'I' to dedicate itself to a deep perception of the other. 'Man is there, in front of us, and we can look at him in slow motion ... in order to verify the concreteness of the moments of his presence to indicate to us the concreteness of our moments of absence.'[14] The film camera must be able to capture the 'specks of dust' of human presence.[15]

Defined by Bazin as the Proust of the present indicative, Zavattini wanted to make material and concrete the simultaneity of perception and thought, rather than represent these phenomena.[16] The means of cinema, he declared, can photograph 'what we are thinking in the act of our seeing it'.[17] Its dimension is that of 'duration' and is realized in the *performance* of the shot, without being constrained by a before (the script) or an after (the editing). In this undertaking the senses, body, action, thought, word and intellect were inseparable.

Moving in an apparently opposite direction to that of Eisenstein, Zavattini draws similar conclusions, attributing to the cinema the same capacity to overcome the duality of sense and reason, by immersing 'the abstract process of thought in the fervor of practical activity'.[18] When, in the early 1960s, he spoke about the hand-held camera, *à propos* of the project of *Diary of a Man*, he meant to indicate a way of shooting capable of expressing the fluidity and leaps of a thought in progress, as attached to things as perspiration is to the skin.[19]

The materiality of the image

'Analytical cinema' sought to be a sort of autopsy of the living body of reality. The film camera must be used like a scientific

14 Zavattini, 'Il cinema e l'uomo moderno [1949]', *Neorealismo ecc.*, 63.

15 Zavattini, '"Carte" di Zavattini 1 [1962]', *Diario Cinematografico*, ed. Valentina Fortichiari, Milan: Bompiani, 1979, 331.

16 André Bazin, 'Cesare Zavattini ou le néo-réalisme italien', *Radio-Cinéma-Télévision* 85, 2 September 1951, 4–6.

17 Zavattini, 'Basta con i soggetti [1950]', *Neorealismo ecc.*, 71.

18 Sergei M. Eisenstein, 'Prospettive [1929]', *Rassegna sovietica* 1 (January–March), 1967, 93–105.

19 Zavattini, 'Carte', *Neorealismo ecc.*, 334, 336.

instrument, to visualize and make us aware of the most hidden particles and their interdependent relations. Their 'almost scientific' purpose was thereby made to coincide with a 'religious' one, in that both have the same spirit of discovery of the world, be it joyous or painful.

On this basis, the image theorized by Zavattini naturally ceases to be a narrative unit, dominated by relations of cause and effect. The shot must no longer be 'the bridge' for the successive shot, he said, but must 'vibrate like a microcosm'.[20] Nor should it be a mould of reality, but rather an operation performed inside reality, its subjective X-ray: 'Each relation with the thing to be communicated is one that implies a *choice* and thus a creative act by the *subject*.'[21] Zavattini knew full well that reality cannot speak for itself, as his detractors often accused him of thinking. Nothing was more foreign to him than the idea of a realism founded on an aesthetic of reflections and of falsely objective reproductions. In fact, his entire literary activity testifies to a rejection of naturalistic mimesis. The accusation levelled against him, that he believed in a neutral and innocent technique dissociated from the ideological choices of the artist, had no substance, especially given Zavattini's formal concern with writing. It was his belief that the cinema constituted a language in which the idealist separation between technique and expression was contradicted by the fact that 'content' was a consequence of style. It was similar to what Luc Moullet and Jean-Luc Godard were to say, namely, that the placement of the camera was already a moral act.

In Italy, the ideas of Vertov and Bazin that were close to those of Zavattini were equally the object of biased and distorted interpretations. There were subtle accords between Zavattini and Vertov on the basis of a conviction they shared that cinema was first of all a means of investigation and experimentation and only secondarily an instrument to represent reality. Aside from their emphasis on film language as

20 Zavattini, 'Il cinema e l'uomo moderno', *Neorealismo ecc.*, 63.
21 Zavattini, 'Tesi sul neorealismo', *Neorealismo ecc.*, 114.

a tool of knowledge, they both attributed the origins of their 'anti-artistic' reflections to the need to oppose traditional aesthetics and its ideology. For both of them this involved a radical distance taken from the narrative and representational conventions that had dominated the cinema and which confined the most modern of the arts to a backwardness compared to the aesthetic revolutions that had been achieved in painting, literature and music.

For Zavattini, images, stripped of the incrustations of traditional aesthetics, returned the image to degree zero. 'It seems to us that we are on the eve', he wrote in 1949, 'of rediscovering the original plastic value of images, what the cinema was the first time a lens was opened to the light of the world. Everything was equal at that time, everything was thought worthy of becoming fixed on a photographic plate. It was the most uncontaminated and promising moment of cinema'.[22]

This operation of stripping the image of its acquired habits led to the celebration of its concrete, sensorial nature. Zavattini almost yearned for brute matter. It was a feature of his writing evidenced by a partiality for oral expression. As Renato Barilli already emphasized in the 1970s, Zavattini opposed his 'event-related' value to the illusory and illusionist nature of images, the living act rather than the represented one.[23]

He projected his experimentalism into the area of materialist and non-figurative art, creating a bridge between, on the one hand, Dada and the avant-garde of the 1920s and, on the other, with the underground and its Happenings and performance practices that had been present from the 1960s.

The physical nudity of Zavattini's images are not far removed from the idea of 'pure cinema' that Bazin had suggested at the end of his 1949 essay on Vittorio De Sica's *Ladri di biciclette*: 'No more actors, no more story, no more sets, which is to say that in the perfect aesthetic illusion of reality there is no more

22 Zavattini, 'Il cinema e l'uomo moderno', *Neorealismo ecc.*, 64.

23 Renato Barilli, 'Introduzione', *Opere di Cesare Zavattini. Romanzi, diari, poesie*, ed. Renato Barilli, Milan: Bompiani, 1974, 9–44.

cinema.'[24] With this paradox of the abolition of cinema, Bazin demonstrated his perfect understanding of the processes of purifying and stripping bare practised by Zavattini. The adjective 'pure' was again suggested, years later and in a similar sense, by Gilles Deleuze who, in his *Cinema 2: The Time-Image*, analysed neorealism in the light of some of Zavattini's ideas. Theorizing the 'pure optical, sound (and tactile) image', Deleuze imagined an image 'possessed by the senses', that is, not based on prearranged actions and characters, but born of an unstructured encounter with reality and possessed of the same sense of solidity, indefiniteness, vitality and lack of cause as reality itself'.[25]

Already in the 1940s, Zavattini was in the strange position of being listened to but often misunderstood with regard, for example, to the later positions taken by the *Nouvelle Vague*, who retraced its origins back to Italian neorealism. The seal of a generous but impressionist and irregular theory was stamped on his ideas, in large part contradicted by its practical applications. Actually, Zavattini's ideas, and he was the first to admit it, placed him in advance of his work as a scriptwriter that necessarily imposed compromises on him while he travelled elsewhere along a more extreme and consistent path. Although in the form of diaries, the dialectical tones of direct confrontation, oral inflection and militancy possessed their own organic quality and even inflexibility. It consisted in always remaining perfectly true to itself, that is, to an idea constantly in process, never defined into formula, and instead devoted to a constant searching in a spirit of disciplined passion.

24 Bazin, 'The Bicycle Thief', What is Cinema?, new edn, vol. 2, intro. Dudley Andrew, trans. Hugh Gray, Berkeley: University of California Press, 2004, 60.

25 Gilles Deleuze, *Cinema 2: The Time-Image*, ed. and trans. Hugh Tomlinson and Roberta Galeta, London: Athlone Press, 1989, 1.

2 *Paisà*: light

Paisà had its premiere at the Venice Film Festival in 1946. It is considered the most emblematic film of neorealism, though the term 'neorealism' was not yet part of critical debate until early in 1948. Rossellini had made his first film in 1939, *Fantasia sottomarina/Underwater Fantasy*, a short film on fish, halfway between a documentary and a fairy-tale. By 1946, he was shooting his sixth feature (that included *Desiderio/Woman*, a film he began in July 1943, completed by Marcello Pagliero late in 1945). He had already enjoyed major success in the United States with *Roma città aperta/Rome Open City* released in Italy in September/October 1945.

Roma città aperta represented a clear sign of a new anti-fascist and liberal period in Italian history. It was a manifesto for a new cinema that seemed to embody all the energy and force of a historical moment. With Rossellini's film, neorealism became the expression of the hopes of an Italy recently freed of fascism and the war. The film adheres to the ideals of the Resistance and exemplified a commitment to the reconstruction of the nation. The idea of a new cinema was closely connected to the idea of a revitalization of Italian society and culture. In the place of, on the one hand, an elite and overly refined art, and, on the other, of an evasive and consolatory one, it provided an art directly involved in the actual experience and problems of Italy.

Roma città aperta recalled events of a recent past that was still current: the German occupation of Rome, the Popular Front of the Resistance that, strongly populist, had unified Catholic and Communist forces. *Paisà* continued in that vein. It evoked a still fresh historical memory of the Liberation and of the role of the Anglo-American forces. From a stylistic point of view, *Paisà* was more experimental and innovative than *Roma città aperta,* still tied to classical schemes of narration. *Paisà* reconnected with the experience Rossellini had making fascist propaganda films in the early 1940s. He had been trained in the school of Francesco De Robertis, a naval officer whose first films as director were *Uomini sul fondo* (1940) and *Alfa tau!* (1942). Both were war films, and though taking place during fascism, refused its rhetorical and celebratory style. Instead, these films favoured everyday aspects of military life. Mixing documentary and fiction, De Robertis shot real-life situations with non-professional actors, though relying on a storyboard to programme every shot. Rossellini benefited from his involvement with De Robertis even if he refused subsequently to rely on what he would regard as the constraints of the script. In contrast, he allowed for a good deal of improvisation in his films. Between 1941 and 1943, he shot his first 'war trilogy' composed of a film on the navy, *La nave bianca/The White Ship* (1941), on the air force, *Un pilota ritorna/A Pilot Returns* (1942) and on the infantry, *L'uomo dalla croce/The Man of the Cross* (1943). In these films, he was already experimenting with the idea of a cinema formally different from the films then being made, an idea whose consequences were destined to be developed after the war and in profoundly different historical circumstances.

The films of the trilogy do not rely on famous stars. Professional actors are mixed with non-professionals. There is an increasing use of documentary material, while staging is reduced to a bare minimum. The films were shot in real-life exteriors in which the stories were embedded. Characters seemed less fictional than men in 'flesh and blood'. The bare and elliptical progression of the story in *Un pilota ritorna* foreshadows the narrative innovations of *Paisà* and its refusal of classical formulas. Rossellini's humanism already had that 'spiritual' quality critics later tended to overlook in *Roma città aperta* and *Paisà*, but finally recognized in *Germania anno zero/Germany Year Zero* (1948), albeit negatively, as a symptom of the director's dangerous deviation from the genuine principles of neorealism and an unfortunate development in his poetics. Nevertheless, despite the ideological barriers and prejudices of some anti-fascist critics, it did not prevent them from recognizing certain fertile signs of a new realist orientation in the propaganda films of the early 1940s. With some embarrassment, it needs to be acknowledged that a great deal of the intuitions that were to guide Rossellini after the war had already been developed in his earlier productions still tied institutionally to fascism.

From project to realization

The genesis of the *Paisà* project has been reconstructed in detail by Thomas Meder, who compared the documents at the Klaus Mann Archive in Munich with all other extant sources. Above and beyond the heterogeneous nature of the material, the multiple versions of the treatment and screenplay, what is most striking in the preparatory stage of the film is the fact that the composition of the crew of scriptwriters was perfectly in tune with the subject of the film. They replicated both the collaboration and the conflicts that are evident in the finished text. An Italian, Rossellini (the director), and an American, Rod Geiger (the producer, ex-soldier, responsible for negotiating sales for *Roma città aperta* in the United States), constituted the team which brought together Sergio Amidei, previously the scriptwriter for *Roma città aperta*, Marcello Pagliero, the communist, Manfredi, in that film, and two foreign writers: the American Alfred Hayes, who had previously worked in Hollywood and was in Italy on a study grant, and the Americanized German, Klaus Mann, son of Thomas Mann, who contributed articles to the United

States Army newspaper *Stars and Stripes* and had fought in the war against his country of origin.

The original title of the project, *Seven from the US*, indicates the initial American focus of the film. Each of the seven planned episodes was to have had an American as its main character, while a prologue provided, in quick flashes, a preview of the characters in the film (in Klaus Mann's version dated September 1945). The first draft of the episodes was to show the Allies advancing from South to North with each of the stories to be set in different parts of Italy. The episode of the American nurse, for example, though unlike the version actually filmed, was initially to have taken place in Naples; the story of the black American soldier and the Italian boy, a petty thief, was to be set in Littoria (Latina); there was no Florentine episode; the North was represented by the Val di Susa and later by the Val d'Aosta instead of the Po River Delta. One episode took place in Anzio and, in an intermediate stage of the script, told the story of an American military chaplain lodged in a convent, an event that was later to be the episode in Romagna. There were many other suggestions: 'Il porco di Predappio'/'The Pig from Predappi'), written by Sergio Amidei, and the encounter, set in the Apennines, between a military chaplain and a fascist adolescent, in Mann's September 1945 script as the sixth episode. The episode called 'Il prigioniero' ('The Prisoner'), written by Amidei and Pagliero, set in the Latium hills, in which Aldo Fabrizi was to have the leading role, was never shot. In the materials found at the Cinémathèque Française, the number of episodes had already grown to six: the Sicilian and Roman episodes (written by Hayes) seem very similar to those in the final version; Naples became the setting for two episodes: the one with the black American soldier and the Neapolitan young boy, and the other with the American nurse. The prologue had disappeared, but it was confirmed that each of the six episodes was to end with the death of the American hero and the image of 'a white cross in a military cemetery', as a 'respectful and affectionate tribute to the memory of those Americans who gave their lives for the Liberation of Italy' and as a 'message to their country'.[1]

During the final months of 1945, the cooperation between the Italian and American scriptwriters fell apart because of internal disagreements. Mann, in particular, contested some of Amidei's ideological formulations, such as the representation of the German rapists in the Sicilian episode, that Rossellini, equally at odds with both writers, would later omit. In the meantime, Rossellini enlisted Massimo Mida and Federico Fellini, and decided to work with them. With Fellini, in particular, Rossellini would write scenes on the set during shooting that had either not been in the script or were differently written. The huge task of preparing *Paisà* (a title probably suggested during the shooting of the Neapolitan episode) was based on a mixture of various voices whose disagreements were often only resolved while shooting as Rossellini came into direct contact with the material of the *mise en scène*. His work method, which influenced the 'modern' style and the practices of the *nouvelles vagues* of the 1960s, was based on the primacy of filming over the script. All the episodes were finalized as they were being shot. The various episodes, neither altogether true nor entirely invented, as Rossellini himself said, issued from a specific relation between actors and setting.[2] The first episode, for example, while not too different from the structure envisaged in the script, was entirely constructed around the protagonist, Carmela Sazio, a poor fisherman's daughter, discovered by chance during a scouting for locations in the Neapolitan hinterland. On the basis of her savage and almost primitive physicality, Rossellini constructed a new history lesson in which Americans and Germans no longer confronted each other as good and bad, liberators and rapists, but rather as two sides of the same coin. Both were manifestations of the *other*, of the foreigner who had landed in a strange land

1 'Il prigioniero', *Cinema Nuovo* 57 (25 April) 1955: 93.

2 Roberto Rossellini, *My Method. Writings and Interviews*, ed. Adriano Aprà, New York: Marsilio, 115.

with an unknown culture. The episode of the monks, even if freely using ideas from the preparatory script stages, was completely invented during the shooting, when the convent was discovered by accident in Maiori. It was the place, according to Rossellini's version, but denied by Fellini and Geiger, where the German prisoners who were used as actors in the Sicilian episode had taken refuge. Likewise, the Florentine episode was written in Naples, with the help of Vasco Pratolini, during the shooting of the story of the black soldier and the child, while the final episode, set in the Po River Delta, was given its final draft in Florence. Such work was done in stages, day after day, sketched out, then filled in, then modified once more during shooting.

There was an atmosphere of legend that surrounded the filming, according to those who took part in it and precisely because the filming was based on chance occurrences. The anecdotes that were told, even taking into account exaggerations and contradiction – Rossellini and Fellini, famous for stretching the truth, were often labelled as incurable 'liars' – revealed the duality being played out between cinema and life. When the Neapolitan episode was being filmed, for example, Rossellini and some of his collaborators on the film were taken into custody in a police round-up reported in the press. They were arrested along with local criminal underworld figures with whom they associated to better discover the underbelly of the city. Those same *guappi* later appeared as extras in the little marionette theatre of the Neapolitan episode. No one better than Fellini, perhaps, knew how to describe that 'spiral of life and invention, observation and creativity' that was a part of the shooting of *Paisà*.[3] In his recollections, Fellini said that, following Rossellini across Italy, he discovered that cinema could be made with the same 'freedom' and 'nonchalance' with which one can draw or write, like 'a marvellous adventure of living and storytelling

3 Federico Fellini, quoted in Giovanni Grazzini (ed.), *Intervista sul cinema*, Roma-Bari: Laterza, 1983, 57.

at the same time,'[4] without any break between them, as if one was 'at the same time spectator and actor, puppet master and puppet, and a special correspondent living the events being reported, like circus people who live in the same ring where they perform and in the same carriages in which they travel'.[5]

Paisà is a structure under constant construction, a 'continuous *happening* between life and the representation of life',[6] according to Fellini, who saw Rossellini place himself 'in an intangible yet clear position between the indifference of detachment and the awkwardness of adherence', where reality can be seen simultaneously from within and from without, as witnessed and as narration.[7] The term 'reality' must be linked not to the so-called objective world but to a dynamic perceptual relation between subject and object. In effect, there is a deeply inherent relation between the subject who speaks about the world and the world as recounted, between experience and narration. The perceptions of Rossellini imposed themselves against conventional representational formulas. The realism of *Paisà* moves in a phenomenological light, emphasized by Amédée Ayfre and André Bazin. It is the film-maker who is close to things and gives the impression of setting these in motion in the narrative rather than bending things to fit a premeditated design.

The neorealist aesthetic, of which Rossellini was the principal representative, did not believe that things 'speak for themselves', as has often been said. Bazin's model of 'restitution' and 'transparency' was a formal model founded on precise stylistic codes. So-called 'reality' in the cinema is the result of an artistic operation, as Bazin and Rossellini both knew. In his 1948 essay 'An Aesthetic of Reality: Cinematic Realism and the Italian School of the Liberation', Bazin declared that 'realism in art can only be achieved in one way

4 Fellini, *Fare un film*, Turin: Einaudi, 1980, 46.
5 Grazzini (ed.), *Intervista sul cinema*, 57.
6 Fellini, *Intervista sul cinema*, 55.
7 Fellini, *Fare un film*, 46.

– through artifice'.[8] Rossellini echoed him: 'to get realism, you need "tricks"'.[9]

Bodies and voices

The life and concrete presence of bodies and things contrasts with codes of verisimilitude and naturalism without, however, entirely effacing them. A preference for direct experience, both visual and sound, exists side by side with representational 'tricks' and deceits, for example, and perhaps pre-eminently, the work by Rossellini on sound and dialogue. *Paisà* adopts a compound approach, mixing live shooting with dubbing, authentic voice material with a life-likeness of it. According to statements by Massimo Mida, the film was shot entirely in direct sound, but at the mixing stage it was necessary to remedy incorrect or confused and poorly recorded sounds.[10] It resulted in an alternation of live and dubbed sound not only in single scenes, but sometimes in the same shot. In that case dubbing was 'suffered' out of necessity. Another issue, though one not involving technology, was the provision for dubbing before shooting; in other words, accepting the idea of dubbing, as occurred in some special instances. Narrative needs – often in contrast with reality – caused Rossellini to have the Neapolitan monks speak in the dialect of the Romagna, which provoked disapproval from a critic like Francesco Callari, who, in his negative review of the film at the Venice Festival, complained about the use of the voices of professional actors such as Carlo Ninchi and Tino Scotti (confusing the latter, perhaps, with Carlo Romano).[11]

8 André Bazin, 'An Aesthetic of Reality: Cinematic Realism and the Italian School of the Liberation', *What is Cinema?* vol. 2, ed. and trans. Hugh Gray, Berkeley: University of California Press, 1972, 26.

9 James Blue, 'Interview with Rossellini (1972)', in Rossellini, *My Method*, 216.

10 Massimo Mida, 'Sei mesi da aiuto', in Adriano Aprà (ed.), *Rosselliniana. Bibliografia internazionale. Dossier 'Paisà'*. Ente Mostra Internazionale del Nuovo Cinema, Rome: Di Giacomo Editore, 1987, 138.

11 Francesco Callari, 'Il buon senso', *Rosselliniana*, 151–152.

Carmela's Sicilian dialect was probably an artificial construction added at post-production. Despite all this, the effect was that of a kind of Babel recorded 'on the spot'. No one seemed to speak the uniform and conventional language expected by the average Italian viewer accustomed to pre-war films. In *Paisà*, dialect and local accents were mixed with American English, British English and German.

This polyphony was part of the exploration Rossellini envisaged for his journey through Italy and was profoundly linked to his idea of history. The immediacy of the authentic clashed with difficulties of communication between different races, cultures and individuals, trapped into a web of mutual incomprehension and immobility. In contrast to Luchino Visconti, who created a universe of dialect composed of archaic and mythic resonances in *La terra trema* (1948), which he made appear as an enchanted closed poetic language, Rossellini, characteristic of neorealism, sought to broaden the area of communication of the cinema by making *Paisà* a point of encounter and difference between various ethnic groups, classes, cultures, languages and speech. This multiplicity became a multiculturalism in the film related to the forces engaged in the relations of liberators–liberated, occupiers–occupied.

Rossellini's exploration was more anthropological than a critical reflection on recent history. For this reason, objections made by Marxist critics or, more generally, by those on the Left at the time concerning his idea of history and his interpretation of events, were often irrelevant and flawed by preconceptions. On the other hand, and despite frequent spiritualist positions in *Paisà*, history in the film did not unfold as a struggle between good and evil, nor as providential design or divine punishment, but primarily as human suffering. The film did not aim at a systematic historiography, but rather sought to show the effect of historical circumstances on the life of individuals. Though steeped in a messianic notion, Rossellini's idea of human sacrifice that accompanies historical change was entirely absorbed by a solitude that was purely secular and by the incomprehension and anti-heroics of anonymous 'poor wretches' who experienced the events of history in the film as exclusively natural occurrences. The fact of persons and the environment still being in a state of upheaval gave the film a quality of a witness to circumstances without the filters of reflection and narrative. As Bazin argued, *Paisà* privileges the dimension of the word over writing, not only in the sense of favouring very particular linguistic idioms opposed to artificial ones created by scriptwriters, but also because, by rejecting the existing rules of dramaturgy, they were also rejecting those of historical reconstruction and narration.[12] The impact of the oral-verbal dimension in the film appeared as documentary material even though the documentary effect was due to artifice and manipulation inherent in all artistic operations. Rossellini, with exemplary ease, took full liberties with respect to history and classical narrative. The industrial weakness of Italian post-war cinema allowed him to work as if he were a pioneer and independent, even though he had a relatively large budget that he managed to secure by his enterprise and somewhat free and easy ways. In fact, it was precisely the richness of the means of production that made the search for 'impoverished' experiences possible. It allowed him, thanks to lengthy shooting schedules (six months), to improvise and continually modify the initial project.

Particular attention was paid to the selection of the actors. Rossellini gave priority to the nature of the body with respect to the way in which an actor appeared. From his point of view, the choice of someone to play a role – preferably a non-professional – was more important than his direction of the actor on the set. The character was determined by his or her physical presence, human and social type and emotional impact. It was also an element in altering the way in which the narrative was told if the presence of an actor might lend itself to unforeseen consequences, as was the case of Carmela Sazio, who shifted the focus of attention from the staging

12 Bazin, 'An Aesthetic of Reality', 97.

of the scene to herself becoming in the process a sign of a femininity that was instinctive, primitive and animal-like. Carmela Sazio was also the first victim, as Mida indicated, of the neorealist myth of an actress from the street, who became incapable of readapting to her position as the daughter of a poor fisherman, once having experienced that 'other place' of cinema. Her partner, Robert Van Loon, was an American soldier, 'the son of butchers from a large farm in America's Deep South', with whom the girl established an affectionate and close relation on and off the set. The three Germans in the Sicilian episode were prisoners whom Rossellini managed to borrow from the American Army, together with eight US soldiers, a tank, three Jeeps and rifles.

Alfonsino Bovino, the Pascà character in the Neapolitan episode, was discovered directly on site and was preferred to Vito Annicchiarico, the child from *Roma città aperta*, whom Rossellini had initially brought with him from Rome. Dotts M. Johnson, the black MP, was, instead, one of the actors (or presumably so) that Rod Geiger had brought from the United States together with Gar Moore (the American soldier in the Roman episode), Harriet White (the nurse in the Florentine episode), Bill Tubbs (the Catholic chaplain in the Romagna episode) and Dale Edmonds (the American officer in the Po episode).[13] As in the Sicilian episode, the close relations established between the actors led, in the Neapolitan episode, to a standardization of the dialogue and gestures of the characters they played. Maria Michi, in the Roman episode, was considered an actress only because she had previously appeared in *Roma città aperta*, but supporting her

13 From the moment that a law, however breached, prohibited the employment of American soldiers in Italy, Geiger had to go to the United States to find actors and promised to come back with the likes of Canada Lee or Frances Farmer. Fellini and Rossellini said on a number of occasions that the cast furnished by Geiger included persons who in life had done everything but act or who were amateurs. The American producer, to the contrary, claimed that he had supplied the film with genuine actors, all of whom had theatrical experience. See the interview of 12 December 1986, *Rosselliniana*, 131–133.

there was a disorderly batch of extras who had been recruited in the infamous nightspot, Moka Abdul. The discovery of the Maiori monks was the basis for the Romagna episode, which, aside from Bill Tubbs, envisaged only persons impersonating themselves, including the Jewish and Protestant chaplains. Rossellini chose Renzo Avanzo, his cousin, the son of a maternal aunt, Baroness Antonietta Avanzo, as the male lead of the Florentine episode. One of the film's producers, Renato Campos, appeared in the scene on the terrace, where he impersonated a bizarre spectator of the war with a pair of binoculars, and gave rise, together with the gag with the English soldiers, who were portrayed as tourists, also holding binoculars, to one of the few comic notes that broke up the drama of the Florentine story. Renzo Avanzo actively participated in the structuring of the last episode, which took place where he had fought during the war and where his family owned land. According to Mida,[14] Cigolani was a poacher who, in the past, had helped the partisans, while according to Gallagher he was an employee of the Avanzo family.[15] Rossellini confirmed that he had known him since childhood, when he spent long periods of time at his maternal grandfather's home. He asked the fishermen from Padua, as he had previously done with the Florentine partisans, for help with and their opinion of the dialogue, as well as of the action, in a place that they knew perfectly well since they had lived there in times of peace and of war.

Places in the narrative and in reality

It has been said that *Paisà* was a quasi-documentary journey of discovery of a troubled and cruel Italy that had never before been filmed. The movie camera, it was said, by leaving the studios, which in any case had not yet begun to function, became the most powerful means for getting to know Italy. This was true and false, at least if taken literally. The path of

14 Mida, 'Sei mesi da aiuto', 137.

15 Tag Gallagher, *The Adventures of Roberto Rossellini: His Life and Films* (New York: Da Capo Press, 1998), 201.

the Allied troops, from South to North, from the landing in Sicily to the battles in the Po Delta, did not in every respect take the same path as the film crew. The locations filmed only partially coincided with the actual places of the Allied advance. Even the move from one place to another in the film was fictitious.

In the beginning of the film, archive material of the Allied landing near Gela gave a sense of truth and authority to the Sicilian episode. In fact, the episode was shot in Maiori on the Amalfi coast, while the final shot of the lifeless body of Carmela on the rocks was shot in Anzio. The Romagna episode, the second filmed but the fifth to appear in the film, was also shot in Maiori, in a convent. In that episode, Rossellini did not depend on archive material to establish a sense of the true, but on two shots at the beginning (one a long shot, the other a close-up) of a different convent that seemed to be located in Romagna. In the Neapolitan story (the third episode filmed, but the second in the film), the places of the story and those in reality perfectly coincide, equally true of the Florentine and Po Delta episodes. Naples and its hinterland, endowed with mythical and fable-like associations, functioned as a metaphor for the entire South. This metaphorical role in the Neapolitan episode was unique in the film. The Roman story, the last to be shot, established a typically 'professional' relation between the indoor scenes shot in actual locations and the outdoor ones chosen for their similarity to other areas in Italy, in particular the scene of the arrival of the Allies which was reconstructed in a street in Leghorn because of its proximity to an American military base, which made it possible for the crew to borrow the tanks used in the sequence.[16] Some of the indoor locations were reconstructed in the studio, at the Capitani Film studios on Via degli Avignonesi, which Rossellini had already used for scenes in *Roma città aperta*.

The practice of combining the real, either with a likeness of it found elsewhere or with a studio reconstruction, was

16 Mida, 'Sei mesi da aiuto', 137.

typical in the industry. The staircase crowded with people in the Florentine episode in which Giulietta Masina appears, for example, took place in the building where Fellini lived. Basilio Franchina recounted that he was entrusted by Rossellini, upset by the death of his son, Romano, to shoot 'a few matching shots' in August 1946, when the film was at the editing stage. The murder of the fascist in the Florentine episode was filmed at the Scalera studios; the guard tower of the Germans and the next to last shot of the Po episode (that of the bodies thrown into the water) was filmed on the Tiber near Fiumicino and used stuntmen. The places portrayed not only have a realistic feel to them, achieved by a variety of means, but also a symbolic connotation that critics, over time, did not fail to grasp.

From the settings in *Paisà*, no matter fictitious or real, figures emerged that forced any reading of the film to go beyond a simple documentarism, the central and most frequently remarked quality of Rossellini's work. Its symbolic charge, however, was an integral part of the documentary surface of the images, as if the two were interdependent. The Sicilian episode evoked a primordial and imaginary place only marginally touched by history. It was viewed through the eyes of foreigners, Americans and Germans, wandering around lost as if on another planet not yet subject to modern civilization. The dilapidated tower with its trapdoor and staircase was a heap of ruins with 'gothic' caves that could only be described by clichés from the literature of the fantastic and of adventure, tales of Frankenstein or of pirates. The dense darkness that everyone except Carmela complained of contributed to the mysterious atmosphere. The darkness contained an ancestral sediment that recalled the mists of time, the night-time of humanity, the world still immersed in chaos, mankind still lost in its own unconsciousness. Tag Gallagher speaks of the ruined interior of the tower as a uterine cavity.[17] The only creature at ease in the tower is the wild and instinctive Carmela. The coming of light into the

17 Gallagher, *Adventures of Roberto Rossellini*, 187.

dark is an omen of death: light provokes Joe's murder and Carmela is murdered as dawn approaches. The interaction of dark and light, the unconscious and reason, prehistory and history reappears in the Neapolitan episode, which also takes place within a closed mythical, atemporal South, whose barbarism was provoked by the ruinous coming of civilization. The image of the temple in Paestum from archival footage is linked to white crosses for the dead. In the Sicilian episode, the gloomy town square in front of the church was replaced by a sunlit, carnivalesque, almost medieval square in Naples, filled with jugglers, acrobats and fire-eaters, a place open to difference and passing encounters. The dark grotto of the Sicilian episode resurfaced in the Neapolitan one as the puppet theatre where the black MP enters, like a giant in the land of Lilliput, as if dropped by mistake into another dimension, like a creature visiting the world of his childhood and with it the unconscious of his own history but as someone different than himself.

The light/dark conflict set against the black/white contrast of the two main characters functions as a rhyme and resonates with the opposition small/large. The child and black soldier couple is like that of David and Goliath, with the Neapolitan petty thief an Orpheus guiding the black soldier into the underworld of the dead. The Pied Piper of Hamelin has a presence, since the episode takes place not in a mythical world but in one of myth turned fairy-tale.

The puppet theatre, in the shape of a dark cavern and animated by the hallucinations of the drunken black soldier, resonates with another cavern, one more terrible, in which the unconscious of the individual becomes vertiginous, reabsorbed into a kind of unconscious of history, swarming with souls confined to the underworld. The grottos in Mergellina inhabited by displaced persons, orphans and all the wretched victims of war and destitution acquire, as Sandro Bernardi notes, a Homeric and Dantesque hellish dimension by their excessive reality, in their living daily in a hereafter, in the true underground of civilization. In the Roman episode, the places suddenly seem prosaic, no longer enchanted. The city squares are all the same, says Fred, incapable of rediscovering his love that has become a mere shadow. Even the women no longer recognize themselves. Everything is played out on the contrast between the memory of a charmed world of a lost romance, and the abject present. The lower middle-class interior of Francesca's home where the love story between the innocent Roman girl and the young foreigner was ignited is contrasted with the squalid interior of the room rented by the hour and with the raucous nightspot in the cellar. These settings are in turn placed against the day of the Liberation with its sunshine and flowers. Six months later, the scene is the streets of Rome at night, where nobody recognizes each other, and the final scene of the morning rain that punctuates the greyness of people's lives. The gaps of space and light reflect something more severe: the disappointment of the American soldier, when, having left his tank (another dark cavern) as a triumphant hero greeted by the crowd and receiving as his reward the virgin of his dreams, he can no longer find the geographical and human coordinates of that brightness of the Liberation, while the city, surrendering to the extinction of hope, has lost its own sense of the future. Only six months had passed and the Liberation has become little more than an album of memories, a nostalgic flashback.

Instead, in Florence, the inhabitants were in turmoil because the fighting was ongoing and fiercely contested. The scene is early August 1944, two months after the Liberation of Rome and four months before the incidents recounted in the previous episode. There is a sense of myth in the air, of adventurous gestures linked to the nowhere inhabited by Lupo, the chief of the partisans who in fact never really existed. What we see, in contrast to the *relived* history in the Roman episode and the history *suffered* in the Sicilian one, is finally history *participated in*, where characters enter the scene as vectors of movement within the interior structures of the surroundings. The Renaissance city, rationally laid out, is the theatre of a historical drama that is manifested first of all as a spatial one by its division into zones: those of the Nazis, those conquered by the partisans and those left untroubled by the Allies. Rossellini represented Florence as a chessboard, a theory of perspectives, passages, barriers to be razed, spaces rent by light and shadows and seen from above, voids rather than fullness. The most frequent view is through binoculars (by the English soldiers, by the former Italian officer who observes the action from his terrace, as a game), from the heights of the gallery windows of the Uffizi and from rooftops. The sense of drama is made exciting by the dizzying perception of something inanimate that envelops the city in a kind of metaphysical stillness. The war reveals itself in the emptying out of spaces, in the painful aspect of the Vasarian passage, with its works of art in crates and the strips of sunlight rhythmically piercing the windows disturbing the gloom. The crossing of the city by Harriet and Massimo is an uninterrupted succession of doors, stairways, grottos, roofs, halls that create a pattern of inactivity (ironically staged by the British soldiers), leading to action and an encounter with death, the bloody deaths of the fascists and of the partisan, the latter in the shape of a Pietà and in Harriet's cry 'My God', a prelude to the cry of Ingrid Bergman's at the close of *Stromboli* (where even Harriet's flowered dress seems to announce that of Bergman's).

In the Romagna episode, the narrative seems to come to a halt once again, no longer in a flashback as in the Roman episode, but at the threshold of a convent. The enchantment that Rossellini tried to depict is of pastoral harmony, an Arcadia, portrayed in the creature-like communion between friars and chickens, marked by the festive rhythms of the bells and stylized in the playful, infantile dances of the monks who run and jump through the ancient rooms of the convent. But in that world, however softly serene and innocent it seems, and however much the walls of the monastery and its faith serve as a refuge from the barbaric acts of history and where blessedness is attained through isolation, echoes of the world conflict nevertheless burst in upon it in the figures of three military chaplains of different faiths (Catholic, Protestant and Jewish). Their arrival into the peaceful small world of the convent sets off the only war that the monks know how to wage: that of faith, of religious intolerance. The Arcadian space becomes a place of conflict furrowed by expressive shadows, the source, for Rossellini, of a wondrousness, however, not without its problems. While suspending judgement, Rossellini represented Arcadia as the place of the film's most heated ideological conflict, shifting conflict from the external world to the interior one and thereby emphasizing its obduracy. The Romagna episode, together with that of the Neapolitan, put into play a dynamic linked to difference (class, race and religion) not exhausted by current history but existing prior to it and subsequent to it, destined to be projected into the present.

In the final episode, the war abandons a closed world of ideas to manifest itself once again as history taking place. But, with respect to the Florentine episode, the scene recalls a primitiveness similar to that in the Sicilian episode, an elemental nature, composed almost exclusively of sky, water and earth, marked by a lack of distinction between animal and vegetable, and by the alternation of day with night. The most common figure is the horizontal line, an almost amphibious point of view that substitutes for the vertical sense of ascension and fall that governs the depiction of the Sicilian tower and Florence, lost in infinite space, without perspectives and void of any topographical orientation. This elemental nature became the stage of a tragic epic, where boundaries between life and death were overlaid with those of day and night and with history and acts of sacrifice on which the waters opened and closed. It was as if in this journey outlined by *Paisà* from the unconscious to the conscious, an ancient horror remained within all understanding and inside the most noble acts.

In the first episode, the Allies could not be distinguished from their enemies. They were confused together in a sort of original darkness. Light appeared as the harbinger of understanding and of death. In the final sequence of the last episode, it was again the border between night and day that ratified the unhappy passage of history. Over the figuration of the water that had just swallowed up the bodies of the partisans, the neutral voice of the narrator injected a vision of a future liberation but one not given to be seen. As in *Roma, città aperta* and *Germania anno zero*, Rossellini ended the narrative with a sight of a sacrificial victim, entrusting the idea of a regeneration with death capable of opening paths towards a 'better future' to a place beyond the film. The slowly diminishing whirlpools of the river in the final scene of *Paisà* evoked an indifferent nature that accepted and absorbed the pain of existence destroyed by time. A sense of circularity, rather than of linear progression, is supported by the image of the water that transports the Allied liberators at the beginning of the film and then swallows up the bodies of the partisans at its close, a circularity equally true in the structure of this final episode. Rossellini was able to use the material symbolically, beyond what was denoted by the structuring of oppositions: outside/inside, above/below, full/empty, close/distant, shadow/light. Such oppositions were the basis of the narrative structure of the film and informed Otello Martelli's cinematography. By his use of chiaroscuro contrasts within a single shot or between shots, Martelli visually exemplified the duality of the real and the symbolic in *Paisà*. He adopted an objective documentary approach which was at the same time expressionist. With his obsessive professional sense, in apparent contrast to Rossellini's cursory methods, Martelli helped to bridge the gap in graphic terms between the physical and metaphysical at the inner core of the film. The struggle between light and dark thereby moved from the merely technical to the semantic.

Archival images and narrative images

Fragments of archive footage with a commentary in the style of a newsreel introduced and linked the various episodes of

Paisà.[18] It was their function not only to provide a histori-cal-documentary frame for the events recounted, but also to move the narrative system of the film in the direction of current affairs reporting. The images taken directly from reality reacted almost chemically on reconstructed ones and, by their contiguity and similarity, functioned to attest to the reality of these. The fictional images at the beginning of the film arise naturally, without any documentary interruption. In the second insert, which precedes the Neapolitan episode, the two categories of images, documentary and fictional, are woven together so closely in a cross-fade that it is difficult to identify where the archival material ends and the fictional story begins. The fact that the voice of the narrator ceased just before the narrative story commenced further contributed to this cohesiveness.

The introduction of the Roman episode is longer and more heterogeneous than the use of archival material elsewhere in the film because in this case there is a discontinuity between story and document. The images of reality and those of the fiction are no longer contiguous but are separated by a gap in time. The archival material must by itself, thereby, function as evidence because the narrative takes place at a distance in time from the historical events of the liberation of Rome. The function of the archive material is to record the effects of those events and re-evoke them when necessary. One inter-title ('Six months later'), the only one in the film, marks this gap in time, as does a musical beginning with 'La canzone del piave', fading into boogie-woogie brought by the Ameri-cans to liberated Rome.

The fourth appearance of archival material occurs during the Florentine episode. Its use is once again marked by the simultaneity between document and story, in the voice of the speaker which, for the first time, is heard over the fictional images, thus breaching the border between reality and its reconstruction. In the Romagna story there was also a similar

18 The voice belongs to Giulio Panicali, who also dubbed Renzo Avanzo in the Florentine episode.

presence of archival material just prior to the fictional story and in different areas: the use of sound where the noise of battle suggests a continuity between story and document, outside and inside, the world of war and the world of peace. The hissing of artillery shells, for example, soon yields to the sounds of the bells of the monastery, the regulated rhythms of an isolated community, though not protected from the inroads of history.

The sixth episode is the only one without an introduction. The sole trace of archival material is the voice of the speaker, who comments on the first and last images, as if they are images of reality and as if document and fiction are in perfect accord. The tone is descriptive and impersonal as it is elsewhere in the film.

Purely denotative, the voice-over accompanies the images throughout the film. At times it simulates the present as live reporting. At other times it re-evokes the past. In other words, it is at once in the midst of events and distant from them. The function of the narrative voice-over is to provide a linear order to the course of the German retreat and advance of the Allied armies. The narrator almost always provides dates for events and precise geographical details that help to situate the six stories. The archival material is crucial to the narrative structure, providing it with an outline and point of reference. Aside from lending the episodes a documentary status, it binds them into a coherent whole as if they are but fragments of a single unity. Thus, the speaker not only provides a neutral and illustrative commentary and also connects the episodes, but is the guide for the journey in *Paisà*, the one who plans its stages and the apparent architect of its design.

The structures of the narration

The originality of the narrative construction of *Paisà* was highlighted by French critics at the time of the film's release. André Bazin and, before him, Georges Altman, compared its cine-journalistic technique with the dry, direct style of American literature of the 1930s and 1940s (John Steinbeck, Erskine Caldwell, Ernest Hemingway, William Faulkner). Bazin, in particular, greeted *Paisà* as the foundation of an 'absolutely new genre' that re-elaborates the form of episode films and thus establishes itself as a 'collection of cinematographic short stories, the exact equivalent of the most modern works which recall the major authors of American short stories'.[19]

Brunello Rondi began his 1956 analysis of the film with the following: 'It would be extremely wrong to consider *Paisà* an episode film.' He later added that the 'breathing' of *Paisà* is 'what is least fragmentary and rhapsodic about it'.[20] The metaphor of breathing perfectly lends itself to the organic composition of the work. The way the film breathes coincides with its syncopated rhythm, which presides over both the succession of shots in each episode and of the episodes to each other. The structural unity of *Paisà* is due primarily to its narrative technique, not to the nature of subject of the episodes, that is, to a stylistic rather than a thematic unity. 'A film, even before being a story, is a rhythm', declared Rossellini in 1946.[21] His gaze always favoured the whole over detail and sacrificed logical connections between shots. His films moved forward using sudden syntheses rather than an analytic series of cause and effect. Assuming that the ellipse is the key figuration for Rossellini, he depletes the language of the film almost to the point of incomprehensibility and stamps the images with an emotive movement which, rather than a gradual crescendo of tension, the traditional construction of a climax, depends on a sudden rupture of the narrative phrasing, on an unexpected appearance of the facts. A continuous sense of vertigo strikes the spectator, disoriented by the story and made to accept conclusions without the slightest explanation or preparation. Perhaps it is by means of such startling rhythm of continual jumps that Rossellini

19 Bazin, in *Le Parisien Libéré*, 1 October 1947.
20 Brunello Rondi, *Il neorealismo italiano*, Parma: Guanda, 139.
21 Roberto Rossellini, 'L'Homme et la liberté', *Paris–Cinéma*, December 1946.

1 *Paisà*. The Sicilian episode: Robert Van Loon (Joe) and Carmela
Sazio (Carmela)

2 *Paisà*. The Neapolitan episode: Dotts M. Johnson (Joe) and
Alfonsino Bovino (Pasquale)

3 *Paisà*. The Florentine episode: Renzo Avanzo (Massimo) and Harriet White (Harriet)

4 *Paisà*. The Po Delta episode

wants us to feel 'the heartbeats of mankind', and make the accelerated or obstructed breath of existence emerge from beneath the surface of stories sketched rather than finished according to the rules.[22] That sense of incompleteness, swiftness, amazement and incomprehension, which seems to belong more to real life than to its representation, is released by such breaks in the narrative. The strong emotional impact of Rossellini's images derives precisely from this wish to offer itself, above and beyond narrative progression and mediation, as a raw and mysterious part of existence, almost as if it were the 'flesh of the world'. A disregard for conventional links between shots guided Rossellini during shooting and, even more importantly, during editing. In fact, after the film's premiere in Venice, before its theatrical release, Rossellini stripped even more flesh from its bones to make it more elliptical.

The composition of *Paisà* lends itself perfectly to a structural interpretation like the one Eisenstein applied to his *Battleship Potemkin* (1925).[23] When *Roma città apertà* was released (1945), critics cited the Soviet film as an example of a cinema related to that of Rossellini's. *Paisà* possesses, like *The Battleship Potemkin*, a great deal of historical content, is considered emblematic of an era, proposes the same profound weave of document and fiction, improvisation and construction, reportage and symbol. The organic nature of its composition is due to the dynamic of conflicts in the story that guides both the structure of the individual parts – the episodes and also the smaller segments within them – and their organization into a unitary complex. *Paisà* moves forward by accelerations, pauses, unexpected setbacks, sudden arrests. The resonance between its parts and their opposing dynamic is evident and permits the highlighting of a system of intersecting rhymes and structural reflections.

22 Ibid.

23 See Sergei M. Eisenstein, *Nonindifferent Nature: Film and the Structure of Things*, trans. Herbert Marshall, Cambridge: Cambridge University Press, 1988.

In all of the episodes the characters are in search of some-thing: Carmela wants to find her father and brother; Pascà, lacking affection, tries to procure enough to live on through trickery and petty thievery; Fred is looking for Francesca on all the streets and squares in Rome; Harriet is hunting for Lupo and Massimo wants to be reunited with his family; the three American military chaplains are looking for a place to spend the night; the partisans with the Americans in the Po Delta are seeking to recover the dead and find some food.

The first three stories are constructed on a pair of charac-ters, one American, the other Italian, who have problems of communication and identification. Within each couple, each individual at a certain point isolates themselves from the surrounding world in a discussion that reveals their inner-most thoughts: Carmela and Joe at the 'large window'of the tower in ruins with the sea in the background; the child and the black soldier sitting on the ruins of bombed-out houses; Fred and Francesca in her house, revisited in a flashback by the drunken American while he is lying on the bed in a room rented by the hour where Francesca has brought him. The dialogue refers to feelings of affection and nostalgia for something far away, lost or absent.

In the three later episodes, there is a shift from the indi-vidual to the collective. The protagonist is a group, even if the director highlights within the group an Italian-American couple: Harriet and Massimo in the Florentine episode, the Catholic chaplain and the Father Guardian in the Romagna episode, Dale and Cigolani in the Po Delta one.

All the episodes end, rather traditionally, in a rhetori-cal flourish of music that is brought to a pathetic peak from outside the fiction in the space of the commentary. It contrasts with the spare aspect of the images juxtaposed to the indifferent voice of the narrator, prepared at any moment to pick up the thread of the narration and introduce the next stage of the journey.

A narrative device, typical of myths and fairy-tales, that recurs in many of the episodes, is that of fated new encoun-ters between the characters, a network of romantic coincidences and failed identifications. Joe finds Pascà again in the chaotic Neapolitan streets after the boy has stolen his shoes, but fails to recognize him at first. Francesca, who has become a prostitute, runs into Fred by chance and does not immediately recognize him. Fred, in turn, will never manage to recognize her. In the midst of the crowds in Florence, Harriet encounters Massimo, a providential 'helper' for the exploit she has decided to undertake. To the conventional-izing tendency of the narrative must be added the typicality of certain characters and scenes: the American soldier, the son of a Sicilian father who was born in Gela; the romantic scene between between Joe and Carmela overlooking the sea, with shooting stars overhead; the drunken black soldier who warbles like a bird; the three females (wild peasant, corrupt *petit bourgeois*, the enterprising, modern American intellec-tual). Such stereotypes are moderated and redefined by the fact that the characters have been placed in atypical and often violently upsetting situations.

Of the six episodes, three represent the war as it is taking place and three represent its consequences. The war episodes are positioned respectively at the beginning (Sicily), the end (the Po Delta) and in the middle (Florence) of the film. Each of these concludes with two or more deaths: that of Joe and Carmela; that of the fascist and the partisan who dies in Harriet's arms; that of Dale and of Cigolani. The first and last episodes are definitely the most elliptical in the film and recall the return to an aquatic figuration. They are the only episodes to portray the Germans in action, though in the Florentine episode they are reduced to silent extras seen from a distance. The three war stories show characters making their way through difficult terrain: the lava channel and the ruined tower; the ghostly, deserted Renaissance city; the marshes infested with Germans.

The other three episodes occur between the war stories as pauses in which reflection follows action, like the aftermath of war, where the problem of living together in peacetime becomes actual. This alternation of war and peace proceeds in counterpoint of soft and loud, like a musical score. With the exception of the Romagna episode, the other two replace the deaths that conclude the war episodes with epilogues of poverty, impotence and hardship. The Neapolitan and Roman episodes end with a similar gesture of an American soldier in the one case driving away in a Jeep dazed by horror, and in the other driven away in a lorry, blinded by disappointment.

Moreover, in the first three episodes of the film, the dialectic between the American liberators and the liberated Italians is marked by mutual mistrust and incomprehension. Beginning with the fourth episode in the Romagna, communication, collaboration and solidarity between the two gradually become more intense, to conclude with the gesture of reconciliation by the American Catholic chaplain, who, moved by the sacrifice of the monks, acknowledges the gulf of understanding between them which will be rhymed in the final episode in the Po Delta when Dale, the American officer, sacrifices himself for the partisans. Above and beyond the echoes, contrasts and structural mirrors, the progression of the episodes seem to suggest, as well, a return of archetypes. The Sicilian episode recalls a mythical story; the Neapolitan one, a fairy-tale; the Roman episode, the romance, or at least its nostalgia; the Florentine episode, the dramatic; the Romagna one, the pastoral; and the episode in the Po Delta, the epic. These genres arise from behind the documentary surface of the images, which works as a filter to bring the two into harmony. The emphasis Rossellini placed on the material of expression both conveys it to the surface and renders it to the depths. The design is almost cosmological. At one and the same time Rossellini lends to the basic and elementary material of existence the palpitations of the present and the immobility of the eternal.

3 *La terra trema*: language

La terra trema premiered at the 1948 Venice Film Festival. It was Luchino Visconti's second film. His first was *Ossessione*, made in 1943 when Visconti was thirty-seven. The film was adapted from James Cain's short novel *The Postman Always Rings Twice* (1934). Visconti was a Milanese aristocrat with an extensive and refined cosmopolitan culture. *Ossessione* was considered a film that broke with the stereotypes of the Italian cinema of the 1930s. It elaborated some of the most vital aspects of Italian culture during fascism: American literature as fostered by Cesare Pavese and Elio Vittorini and the lesson of French cinematic realism, in particular the work of Jean Renoir, with whom Visconti worked as an assistant in the 1930s. His experience working with Renoir (on *Partie de campagne* and *Les Bas-Fonds* (both made in 1936), during the period of the French Popular Front and the war in Spain, was an aesthetically and politically rich experience for Visconti. French cinema was in thrall to the avant-garde with its stylistic innovations, radical political commitments and support for the interests of the working class. It was Renoir who introduced Visconti to *The Postman Always Rings Twice*.

Between the end of the 1930s and the early 1940s, Visconti came into contact with the Italian film journal, *Cinema*, edited by Vittorio Mussolini, son of Benito Mussolini. *Cinema*, paradoxically, became the voice of a new anti-fascist criticism.

It published articles by Michelangelo Antonioni, Gianni Puccini, Giuseppe De Santis, Carlo Lizzani, Mario Alicata, Massimo Mida and Antonio Pietrangeli, and by Visconti. Members of the group were to become film directors after the war or, as with Alicata, a leading member of the Italian Communist Party (PCI). The journal argued in favour of an Italian cinema opening itself to ideas and practices current in Europe, and particularly in French cinema. It emphasized a realism as a counter to the comedies during fascism ('white-telephone films'). It called for abandoning the studios and going outdoors into the Italian landscape. It pointed to the literature by Giovanni Verga and Italian literary *verismo* as a model for the renewal of the Italian cinema. Visconti fully shared the group's passion for Verga. Even before *Ossessione*, he developed the idea for a film based on Verga's short stories and novels.

Ossessione was as much a Visconti film as it was a film of the *Cinema* group and it achieved the objectives espoused by the group for Italian cinema. *Ossessione* was a film-manifesto. It severed itself from the cinema of the past and opened the way for a new cinema, that of Italian neorealism. In the five years between *Ossessione* and *La terra trema*, Visconti actively participated in the struggle for liberation from fascism and the Nazi occupation and for which he was imprisoned. In the immediate post-war period, Visconti worked in theatre, where he staged plays that apparently had little to do with his neorealist poetics in film, though his theatrical productions profoundly changed practices in the Italian theatre. He introduced a new way of working with actors based on Stanislavsky and he gave an expressive-symbolic role to settings and lighting. He was obsessive about the factual, for a *verismo* in detail also evident in his films. With the end of fascist censorship, he brought new plays to the Italian stage (by Jean-Paul Sartre, Jean Cocteau, Ernest Hemingway, Tennessee Williams, Arthur Miller), in which his civic passions and choice of subjects such as incest and homosexuality were evident. In the same year as *La terra trema*, Visconti produced *Rosalinda or As You Like It* by Shakespeare with set designs by Salvador Dalí. It was a production based on spectacle, fantasy and the marvellous that seemed – even to his contemporaries – the opposite of the aesthetic he pursued in film. In fact, *La terra trema* represents an extreme experiment within the framework of neorealism. All its positions seemed to have been literally and rigorously applied: real settings, non-professional actors, social criticism, the set versus the screenplay, the use of dialect.

The origin of the film started as a political documentary on Sicilian fishermen commissioned by the Italian Communist Party. After the work of finding locations, Visconti enlarged the original project. He proposed to investigate three aspects of Sicilian reality – not only the difficult lives of fishermen, but the struggles of miners and peasants. The seemingly incongruous title, *La terra trema*, is what remains of this unrealized project. The 'completed' film narrates events in a town of poor fishermen in Aci Trezza. It brings together documentary with the romantic-melodrama of Verga's *I Malavoglia* (*The House by the Medlar Tree*), a story that revolves around the vicissitudes of the Valastro family (the grandfather, the widowed mother, the sons 'Ntoni, Cola, Vanni and Alfio, and the daughters Mara and Lucia), and which directly inspired Visconti. The grandfather represents tradition and resignation. 'Ntoni personifies the restlessness and revolt of youth that no longer accepts being subjected to the exploitation of the fish wholesalers. He urges the family to free themselves from the wholesalers by mortgaging their house for capital in order to establish their own business. At first, the favourable fishing conditions rewarded their initiative. But one day a storm lashes the Valastro's boat, destroying it. The young men are left without work. The family, oppressed by debts, is forced into foreclosure by the bank and must leave their home. While Cola decides to run off and join a band of smugglers, 'Ntoni returns to the wholesalers to beg for work. Around these events, tied to work and class struggle and symmetrical to them, are sentimental experiences. 'Ntoni courts Nedda, and Mara falls in love with Nicola, a bricklayer. Both couples are to experience the failure of their romantic dreams as the economic conditions of the Valastros worsen. Lucia, instead, like Cola, represents damnation, an inability to resist temptation and the unknown. Her relationship with Don Salvatore, the head of the local police, betrays the values of the family and the tradition that Mara takes upon herself to preserve and protect. Although one of the least studied aspects of the film, the juxtaposition of dialect and standard Italian goes to the heart of Visconti's method of work and the contradictoriness of his aesthetic, a combination of documentary and a highly wrought *mise en scène* subjecting the real to constant transfiguration and Marxist ideology to the lure of myth.

The choice of dialect

By its extremism and rigour, there is nothing comparable to the linguistic choices of *La terra trema*, neither in contemporary neorealist cinema nor in the history of Italian cinema generally, with the exception perhaps of *L'albero degli zoccoli* (1978) by Ermanno Olmi. Fundamentally shot in direct sound, Visconti's 'cherished' and incomprehensible Sicilian has no links with the dubbed Roman in Vittorio De Sica's *Ladri di biciclette* (1948) nor with the plurality of languages of *Paisà*. If, as in these films, it responds to the call for an as-yet-unheard 'Italian vernacular', it departs from them by an elitism and radicalism that, while embracing ideological and aesthetic positions implicit in the use of the vernacular, goes beyond them by an extreme aestheticism.

As the opening titles suggest, the use of dialect is a rejection of the ethnic-linguistic separation in Italy and of the dominant position of Italian.[1] But, in that rejection, rather

---

1 The opening titles read: 'The events portrayed in this film take place in Italy, more precisely, in Sicily, in the town of Aci Trezza, that lies on the Ionian coast not far from Catania. / The story told by the film is the same one heard over and over again in all those places where men exploit other men. / The houses, the roads, the boats, the sea in the film all belong to Aci Trezza.

than closing the gap, it exacerbates it. It does not bring Italy nearer to the dialects at its peripheries, but instead distances these indefinitely, turning socio-cultural isolation into a poetic force. Thus, the closure, the archaism, the impossibility of translation becomes for Visconti objects of aesthetic fascination. He feels the ancient language of Sicily to be 'similar to Greek', a language filled with 'images', something that attracts him to the magic of its sounds and endless evocation of the mythical.[2] 'It should not seem strange', he wrote in 1941, 'that when speaking of an eventual cinematographic production (of *I Malavoglia*), I insist on elements of sound such as the roar of the sea, the sound of Rocco Spatu's voice, or the echo of our old friend Alfio's cart that never stops, because I want to make it clear to you that if one day I am fortunate enough and have the strength to make the film I dream of from *I Malavoglia*, the most valid justification for my doing so will certainly be the feeling that long ago it touched my soul. It left me with the conviction that for spectators like myself, the mere sound of those names – Padron 'Ntoni Malavoglia, Bastianazzo, la Longa, Sant'Agata, "La Provvidenza" – and of those places – Aci Trezza, il Capo dei Mulini, il Rotolo, la Sciara – will serve to open onto a fabulous and magical scene where words and gestures will have the religious importance of the things essential to our humanity'.[3] The men's voices in *La terra trema* become one with natural sounds and the sounds of work, re-echoed in a single musical scene.

Visconti's shots are always resonant: at times they are filled with noise and shouts and at other times marked by meagre

---

All the actors of the film were chosen from among the townspeople: fishermen, farm labourers, bricklayers and fish merchants. They speak in their dialect to express their rebellion, suffering and hope. For in Sicily, Italian is not the language spoken by the poor.'

2 Jacques Doniol-Valcroze and Jean Domarchi, 'Entretien avec Luchino Visconti', *Cahiers du Cinéma* 93, March 1959, 8.

3 Luchino Visconti, 'Tradizione e invenzione', in *Stile italiano nel cinema*, Milan: D. Guarnati, 1941. Reprinted in Lino Miccichè, *Luchino Visconti*, Venice: Marsilio, 2002, 96–97.

sounds, or else invaded by voices coming from outside that stress the depth of the staging of sound. If, on the one hand, this polyphony seems to evoke the inarticulate and confused hum of life and its complex musicality, on the other hand, the words in dialect, sculpted like crystal, carry the full weight of their symbolic power. It is precisely by fixing on the primitive language of his humble speakers that Visconti recovers that 'violent tone, full of imagination, of an epic', that 'intimate and musical rhythm', that 'religious and fatal tone of ancient tragedy' he had heard in *I Malavoglia*, and in Verga's Sicily seeming to him, a 'reader from Lombardy' to be the mysterious 'Island of Ulysses'.[4] In its suggestive sound textures, the dialect of Aci Trezza is, for the director, the object of a literary love affair, even before it is a document of asocial reality. The meticulous and assiduous adherence to the linguistic 'truth' of the Aci Trezza fishermen is overturned, but not negated, by linking it to the mythical. The fascination of the dialect is precisely a fascination with a lost language, an ancient one, whose antiquity gives it irresistible poetic force. That is why, in the transfigured realism of *La terra trema*, it functions more as representation than as document and is more expressionist than it is naturalist. This epic-lyrical feel to the language leads Visconti to use dialect as a musical score that underlines its ritual fixity while exercising careful work on the dialogue that negates any idea of neorealist improvisation or popular spontaneity. The language of the humble fishermen, wrapped in rags like princes in their brocades, is a language carefully chiselled and precious, shaped by Visconti in bringing together his literary culture and the expressive world of the fishermen, not unlike the use of language in Verga.

Working on the dialogue

Visconti shot the film without a screenplay. He would create scenes day by day on the set. 'The film', he wrote in a letter to Mario Serandrei from Sicily once the shooting had begun, 'is

4 Visconti, 'Tradizione e invenzione', 96.

shot not only with real characters but in situations that tend to arise as I keep to a vague subject ... I write the dialogue as things occur, with the help of the interpreters, that is, I ask them *how they would instinctively express a certain feeling, and what words would they use for it.*'[5] This working method is confirmed in the hand-written diaries kept by Francesco Rosi, the assistant director on the film: 'Visconti imposed the dialogue between Cola and 'Ntoni using the usual system of asking them what they would do and then marking down the words for the dialogue they would use to express their ideas about a certain fact.'[6]

Visconti tends, nevertheless, to exaggerate the actual contribution of the interpreters in giving the dialogue a romantic aspect, while he never refers to the fact that it is partially derived from Verga. The literal translation of words and expressions taken from *I Malavoglia* in certain scenes limits the space of invention for the actors, without, however, losing the basic premise of Visconti's method. This is formulated along the lines of a Socratic dialogue of interrogation and provocation, on the one hand on 'suggesting and suggestions' to the actors and, on the other on the director's 'capacity as a diviner' able to grasp and extract the most appropriate colouration and poetic accents from them.[7]

In any case, Visconti's actors work on something more than an open sketch, like a plot outline or what they imagine. Visconti's indications are precise and detailed, as can be seen in notes he wrote on 'Ntoni's speech to the fishermen in which the conceptual structures and the logic of his words are already provided. Visconti takes from the actors

5 'Lettere dalla Sicilia', *Bianco e nero* 1, March 1948, 50.

6 The work diaries are preserved at the Cinémathèque Française in Paris. In this essay we will be using previously unpublished documents placed at our disposal not only by the Cinémathèque Française, but also by the Fondo Visconti in Rome, the Pietrangeli Archives at the City of Cesena Film Center, the Centro Sperimentale di Cinematografia in Rome and by the personal archive of Lino Miccichè.

7 Visconti, 'Cinema antropomorfico', *Cinema* 173–174 (25 September–25 October 1943), 109.

are nothing but beasts [donkeys] of burden', says 'Ntoni or 'Nuàutri semo carni 'i travagghiu, comu 'u sceccu 'i compari Janu,' / 'We are nothing but flesh for toil, like comrade Jano's donkey,' that Cola repeats, echoing in both cases a phrase uttered by 'Ntoni in *I Malavoglia*: 'Carned'asino'; he muttered, 'ecco cosa siamo! Carne da lavoro!' Cola also speaks of 'I cosi storti' / 'twisted, unjust things', Bandiera di 'Supicchiarì' (abuse), and 'Ntoni about ''na cosa fitusa' (something dirty, despicable) to describe the injustice of the brokers, ''sti latri di riattèri' / 'those broker thieves', 'ca ni sfruttanu sempri a nuàutri piscaturi' / 'who always exploit us fishermen', 'ca s'arricchiscunu sulu a 'i nostri spaddì' / 'who just get rich off of us', 'ca ci anu tuttu 'u vuscutu e nuddu arriscu' / 'who reap all the profits and take no risks'.

The scales of the middlemen are 'valanze di Giuda' / 'Judas' scales', as in *I Malavoglia*,[10] and 'Ntoni's revolt that incites the fishermen to join together as a class at various points, is expressed with phrases such as: 'Si semu tutti d'accoddu, 'u sangu non n'u sucanu cchiùi' / 'If we can all agree, they won't suck our blood any more' – which, even out of context, is still an echo from *I Malavoglia* (100, 202); 'Nuàutri nun n'amu a méntiri a paura r'iddi! I primi di nuautri ca 'ncuminciano a travagghiari suli, l'autri si pisshianu di suraggiu e 'nni vènuno appressu! E poi 'nni dicinu ggrazzie!' / 'We don't have to be afraid of them. The first of us that start to work on our own, will give the others enough courage to follow us! And then they'll thank us!'

Phrases act as counterpoints, both bitter and hopeful, to the final declarations of 'Ntoni to Rosa: 'Ma veni 'u iornu ca 'u sannu sèntiri tutti ca iu ci aiu rraggiuni! Allora, a pèrdiri tutti cosi comu mi finiu a mmia, a statu bbeni pi tutti! Bisogna ca n'imparamu a vulirini bbeni unu cu' 'nn'autru, e di èssiri tutti 'na cosa. Allura sì, ca si po' ghiri avanti!' / 'But the day will come when everyone knows I'm right and they will listen

10 Giovanni Verga, *I Malavoglia*, in *I grandi romanzi*, Milan: Mondadori, 1972, 43. From this point on, page numbers will refer to this edition of *I Malavoglia*.

to me! So, losing everything as has happened to me was good for everyone! We have to learn to care for each other and to unite. At that point we can start making progress!'

The *mise en scène* of the dialect

The method of fleshing out dialogue was developed in five stages: first, Visconti detailed an outline of required dialogue; second, he met with the actors and showed them the outline and in return received suggestions, indications, key words; third, he polished that version into the definitive one; then he passed it over to Zeffirelli, responsible for dialogue, costumes and acting, for a translation from the old people in Aci Trezza in order to find the most archaic and poetic expression possible; and, finally, the translated text was adapted to each actor, transcribed again, learned by heart by the actors, who were still under the charge of Zeffirelli. At this point, the dialogue in the text had become established and permanent, ready to be recited before the camera after a number of rehearsals to make it seem as if this was normal speech established at the time the initial screenplay was written.

What emerges from this reconstruction of Visconti's method, confirmed by Rosi, Zeffirelli and the actors, is the formation of a genuine linguistic workshop that, in its first three phases, the inventive one, is Italo-Sicilian, and in the remaining two is purely dialect. The paper on which dialogue was written, whether typed or by hand, confirms this double linguistic exercise and, in some cases, perfectly illustrates the dynamics of passing from Italian, the language in which the dialogue was conceived, to Sicilian, the language in which it is first formulated and then recited. Visconti's linguistic workshop seemed to perfectly correspond to that established for the scenes in the film in which, for example, the house of the Valastro family was not a real place but a combination of three different buildings in Aci Trezza. And, like that house, which has a window opening on two different homes in the town (one for the outdoor scenes and the other for those indoors, which Visconti purposely excavated then walled up again after the film was shot), the dialogue of *La terra trema* is not a language taken from real life, and even less so is it improvised, but an elaborate reconstruction as a result of an encounter between three different linguistic systems: that of Verga, that of Visconti and that of the fishermen. The finalization of this linguistic edifice lasted six months, the same time it took to shoot the film. It was a true 'staging of language' perfectly integrated into the theatricalization of reality by Visconti at other levels of the film.

The recording in direct sound in *La terra trema* is an exemplary orchestration of the aural and the visual, movement and speech, sounds and gestures, settings and characters, all perfectly pre-planned and calibrated almost as if they were 'already edited'. And the actor 'taken from the street', but taught by Visconti, played a fundamental role in Visconti's continuous relation between presence and reciting, naturalism and stylization.

From subtitles to commentary

Reconstructing the genesis of the spoken commentary in *La terra trema* means entering a zone of shadows, silence, pauses. Though there is no existing document that explains when and why it was decided to use the voice of a speaker, it is reasonable to suppose that the problem of a commentary in voice-over was decided only when the film was completed (the voice-over commentary is already present on the print presented at the 1948 Venice Festival: it was an inevitable compromise, a sort of self-imposed restriction owing to the need to make at least partially comprehensible a film whose spoken language was otherwise impenetrable. The voice-over seemed to Visconti marginal to the film, an addition detrimental to the extreme purity of the work expressed in the archaic and untranslatable music of the Aci Trezza dialect. This can also be deduced from the fact that in 1951 Visconti asked Fausto Montesanti (the director of the Cineteca

Nazionale at the time) to cancel the commentary in the screenplay that was obtained and published in *Bianco e nero*. It was as if, after a great deal of misadventures connected to this *film maudit*, at first 'corrupted' by a commentary alien to the original intention of the film, then definitively falsified in the dubbing of a considerably shortened print, *La terra trema* could only retrieve its original and authentic nature in a literary form.

On the other hand, Visconti, who went to great lengths in essays and interviews concerning his aesthetic and ideological attraction to the Sicilian dialect, never made the slightest mention, not even negative, concerning the Italian commentary and, though totally removing it, he spoke of an original print of the film presented in Venice in 1948 with subtitles.[11] The reviews at the time deny this affirmation which, nevertheless, is an emblematic defence of an ideal version of a *La terra trema* that was never released in Italy.

The spoken commentary was written by Antonio Pietrangeli during the summer of 1948. His first draft is certainly later than the original draft of the commentary that opens the film, because it uses phrases which were then modified or suppressed in later versions.

The subtitles, written by Antonello Trombadori, are in its original draft considerably (and inappropriately) longer and more elaborate than the ones that actually appeared in the film and that accounted for little more than a single page out of the original six. We would not insist on the size of the texts and their chronology if they did not cause some suspicion. In other words, Visconti may have thought of resolving the problem of the incomprehensibility of *La terra trema* with the use of single written subtitles, resorting to the practice of inter-titles in silent films rather than using a voice-over speaker as in a documentary style. Such a solution, which must have immediately seemed impractical and inadequate, would have at least avoided interference with the fabric of the sound in the film that Visconti cared so much about. It would

11 Doniol-Valcroze and Domarchi, 'Entretien avec Luchino Visconti', 8.

also avoid the difficulty consequent on the linguistic dualism introduced by the Italian commentary. Our suspicion is
confirmed by the fact that, in the original draft, the commentary was not limited to introducing the film, establishing
the aesthetic and theoretical premises, as if it were a sort
of manifesto of the most intransigent neorealist poetic, but
rather it follows the narrative development by taking up, with
a strong ideological turn, the story of 'Ntoni's rebellion. Not
without rhetorical accents, the text concentrates on his *dream
of revolt,* leaving the other characters in the background, not
mentioning their love stories nor anything not strictly related
to the economic-social-ideological implications of the events
in 'Ntoni's life.

Trombadori's words have an explicitly polemic and mili-
tant tone without any shading. In almost every paragraph,
society is identified as the cause of the injustices shown in
the film.

The Marxist interpretation of 'Ntoni's story does contain
some exemplary passages: 'The price the boat owners pay to
buy the poor fishermen's labour is only good for one thing:
for granting them the minimum necessary for survival, to
give them enough strength to return to sea every evening, to
fish, to bring the catch back to land, almost as if it they were
no longer men but machines without basic human rights.'[12]
And, more explicitly: 'For Antonio and for the hundreds of
poor fishermen from Aci Trezza, the same destiny repeats
itself every day: [turning oneself into merchandise], working
to survive, submitting to injustice, smothering the slightest
ambition or sense of dignity.' Key words like 'merchandise'
already cut from the original screenplay, or expressions like
'machines without basic of human rights', were also destined
to disappear from the spoken commentary that was to replace

12 They refer in parenthesis to words or phrases crossed out by hand, and
substituted for in the original text of the subtitles, in Lino Micciché, *La terra
trema di Luchino Visconti. Analisi di un capolavoro,* Turin: Associazione Philip
Morris Progetto Cinema–Centro Sperimentale di Cinematografia–Lindau,
1993, 229–230.

these portions of the introduction because they were deemed too modern and 'intellectual', and therefore extraneous to the archaic linguistic context of the film which even the voice-over sought to maintain.

Yet, the commentary was often to repeat this lengthy initial text, even if it abandoned its overly rhetorical or assertive tone and some of its impassioned projections and bright optimism. The subtitles at the end of the film read: 'Ntoni 'rediscovers the force to start all over again because he knows that his is a just cause. He takes the oar like a day labourer on the boat of the wholesalers, and accepts his place again in the chain of rowers. But his experience was not in vain: he knows now that in order to break that chain, you need allies, millions of men united as brothers.'

This passionate Marxist gospel is retained almost literally by Pietrangeli in the first draft of the commentary, even if it will remain a bare but essential skeleton in the final version: 'But no one will be able to help him until they all have learned to care for one another and become a unit. It is within himself that 'Ntoni must find the courage to start over again ...' The two lines at the end are decidedly more distant: 'So, starting over again, the Valastros go back to the sea. The sea that is bitter and the sailor who dies in the sea.' Borrowing the final proverb from Verga, the commentary signs off the conclusion of 'Ntoni's story with a mournful note and, with brusque turn, different from the 'Ntoni aware and hopeful in the last shot.

Actually, what is signified in that instance is the Viscontian contradiction at the basis of the film that is also reflected in the voice-over commentary, but in this case with a clear shift towards the ideology of the 'vanquished'. In other words, even the commentary is part of that vital (because dialectical) uncertainty of presenting itself as other and different from the film.

the sea does not even seem the same as the one that seized 'Ntoni's boat.)

NOVEL

[Owner 'Ntoni] 'Buontempo e mal tempo non dura tutto il tempo!,' osservò il vecchio (p. 148). (Good weather and bad weather do not last forever!' the old man observed.)

'I vetri della chiesetta scintillavano, e il mare era liscio e lucente, talché non pareva quello che gli aveva rubato il marito alla Longa' (p. 44). (The windows of the little church glistened, and the sea was calm and shiny, such that it didn't even seem like the one that took away Mrs Longa's husband.)

I Malavoglia has a reserve of colours, shapes, sketches, echoes and ancient words. The commentary performs the same operation on Verga's novel as the film does in relation to dialogue. It assumes the novel is on a par with the reality staged as material subject to manipulation. Yet, their linguistic likeness allows the film commentary to promote its relation to the novel and at a level where there exists no actual correspondence between the visual aspect of the film and its verbal one. This involves adopting Verga's indirect free discourse as the film's basic stylistic ideal.

From the first to the last drafts, the text of the voice-over is progressively modified in order to achieve a simplicity of speech, as if stripped down to reproduce the suggestiveness and forms of dialect. This involves, besides vocabulary, the structures of speech insofar as they are structures of thought.

If the commentary does not manage to make expressive use of Verga's scorn for grammar, it nevertheless resorts to literary expedients that are already present in the novel stylistically, like an anacoluthon (a breach in syntactic regularity) in order to evoke the language of the humble poor. Similarly, it frequently uses the conjunction 'that', whose function is not always easy to identify. It is used variously as causal, final, consecutive, adversative-temporal, pleonastic-adjunctive and emphatic.

It is exploited by Verga both as a conjunction and as a pronoun in diverse ways. It has only a pale echo in the

5 *La terra trema*. Interior of the Valastro house. Agnese Giammona
(Lucia) and Nelluccia Giammona (Mara)

6 *La terra trema*. The women wait for the return of the Valastro boat

commentary in *La terra trema*, where the Italian *che* trans-
lates the widespread *ca* of Sicilian. In Pietrangeli's (and
Visconti's) text, what is lost is that 'fantastic and choral grace'
characteristic of its use in *I Malavoglia*, mentioned by Luigi

7 *La terra trema*. Antonio Arcidiacono ('Ntoni) and the little girl Rosa.

Russo's words, but in which, nevertheless, a popular expressive accent still remains.

Visconti, in this way, sought to create a 'poetic' closeness of the text to reality (the world of the fishermen) and thereby recreate a correspondence between that reality and the film – that is, between two opposite linguistic choices – but with a common expressive core. Where the dialogue in the film goes back to the spoken language of fishermen, having retranslated what Verga had translated from Sicilian into literary dialect, the commentary performs the opposite task, however, in the footsteps of Verga. It imitates the spoken dialect in the form of indirect free speech. In both cases, an anti-literary position becomes an aesthetic ideal, the result of a complex work of formal elaboration, a kind of stylistic sculpting. There is a simplicity to the dialogue that is at the same time true and enigmatic, like certain phrases in the commentary that reproduce the simplicity of popular speech. Both issue from the same expressive tension and together reflect the search for 'authenticity' by means of stylistic transformation.

The typology and functions of the commentary

A Sardinian actor, Mario Pisu, reads the commentary of *La terra trema*. His voice, with its classical and polished sonorities, lacking the inflections of dialect, seems to be like the one speakers normally deploy in Italian documentaries, that is, a voice outside the universe being portrayed, illustrating it, providing the spectator with a key to interpretation and thereby shaping a point of view. Nevertheless, in this kind of documentary, the commentary in voice-over creates evident anomalies and disruptions. Above all, it is superimposed on a story entirely independent of it, as if wanting to open up a closed world, but one, nevertheless, already made complete and self-sufficient. If, on the one hand, the commentary seems structurally unnecessary (to a Sicilian, or one acquainted with Sicilian sounds or by the use of subtitles), on the other hand it provides additional information and meaning that emphasizes, intersects, dilates the original sense of the film, as happens at its conclusion.

Moreover, the linguistic and stylistic aspect of the commentary seem narratively odd insofar as it is both inside and outside the film: *outside* because the narrator does not belong to the diegetic (realm); *inside* because, through indirect free discourse, it partially assumes the features of language and thought of the characters in the story. The point of view of the narrator becomes mixed with that of the characters, whose feelings and judgements are also reproduced by him. The view and perspective on action by the voice-over commentary is privileged rather than being merely narrative or descriptive. Thus, the forms of an ancient language, with its epic and popular cadences, are made to serve an *ideological* function. Strictly adhering to the dialogue of the film, the commentary never interrupts it by modern vocabulary or pronunciation (that is Marxist), which explicitly mentions 'Ntoni's predicament as a story of growing political awareness. In the actual dialogue, however, this political consciousness is underlined, for example, in the encounter between little Rosa and 'Ntoni.

This ideological importance of the discourse of the commentary, even if it becomes dominant in many instances, never appears separate from its other functions: informative, descriptive, explicative, narrative in a strict sense, and as the partial translation of dialogue.[13] This combination of functions is not merely illustrative. It describes without being redundant to the subtitles, narrates more than it describes, adds more than it duplicates, interprets more than it explains. From its first utterance, for example, in the presentation of where the action takes place, it resorts to phrases such as 'as usual', 'like every night', 'from the grandfather, to the father, to the grandchildren, it's always been like that', which indicate the immobilism and ritual aspect of the story. The same thing happens in the subsequent interventions where an epic tone predominates over simple description. Nothing is ever purely denotative; in other words, interpretation always lies within description, decision within explanation. Sometimes the explicative function is even suspended in interrogation, in the commentary related, for example, to the appearance of the stowaway on the slopes of Mount Etna and to Lucia's escape. The narrator, aside from not revealing the shadows that already surround these two episodes, takes the place of a chorus, simultaneously external and internal to the narrated event. In a not dissimilar way in the scene where the wholesalers discuss the revolt of the fishermen, the commentary is both interrogative and exclamatory, and in referring to Nedda's playing with 'Ntoni, the commentary is essentially interrogative, the only instance where narrator turns directly to one of the characters. With the exception of these rare instances, the voice-over is never an intermediary, neither real nor fictitious, and does not physically mix with the other voices of the film. Only in the conversation between Nedda and 'Ntoni does the commentary repeat the last word ('tomorrow') in the conversation between Nedda and 'Ntoni. What seems exceptional, because it is isolated, is the irony in the commentary regarding 'Ntoni's love for Nedda and her closeness to him that the spectator can understand only later on, after having seen the sequence in which 'Ntoni calls

13 For an analytical study of the ideological importance, refer to Micciché, *Visconti e il neorealismo*, 108–109, 169–181.

out for Nedda desperately without a reply after the economic circumstances of the Valastros have altered for the worse.

Partially camouflaged, only in very few cases does the narrator translate conversations directly or indirectly. Sometimes he uses them, without attributing them to the characters, as choral points of view on the action. The words or the sinews of dialogue are derived in many instances from Verga in the interventions by the commentary. Usually, the citations in the dialogue follow their implementation in the film, according to the figure of the thunder (word) that comes behind the lightning (image). But, facing that delayed translation in the dialogue, there is no lack of interventions in which the description and comments on the action precede the action or accompany it, which happens in many cases. Independently of their place in the temporal progression of the story, certain remarks in the commentary provide extra-diegetic information or chronological emphases, not directly evident from the film and thereby superimposed upon it.

The language of prose and the language of poetry

Given that the work on the dialogue had been a difficult path from Italian to Sicilian, the commentary moves in the opposite direction, from Sicilian to Italian, closing a circle to a certain degree and institutionalizing, within the film, a linguistic and cultural contrast that was intended to be left outside it as the opening subtitles indicate:

> All the actors of the film were chosen from among the towns-people: fishermen, farm labourers, bricklayers and fish merchants. They speak in their dialect to express their suffering and hope. For in Sicily, Italian is not the language spoken by the poor.

The commentary is introduced into the film as an authoritative language outside the world represented. It is the same language spoken in works of fiction by bank employees to stowaways, or written on death notices on official bureaucratic paper attached to walls.[14] This ideological–cultural interaction cannot help but have repercussions on the artistic order of the film. Coming from above and beyond the dialogue, it has the effect of compromising the enchantment of the sound. It also seeks to open a closed means of expression, however perfectly such expression is in accord with the world portrayed and is attentive and crucial to its magic. As much as Visconti seeks to find, within certain limits, a stylistic operation similar to that of the film, by resorting to the use of free indirect discourse for epic effect, the commentary inevitably ends up as a version in prose opposed to the essential poetry of the film.

This constitutes a reshaping detached from the story where the chaos of life is experienced and expressed in dialect. It opposes words as rational order to voices as instinctive disorder, that of an ancient language not yet separate from the physical nature of 'pure' existence. It emphasizes the reflexive moment opposed to the expressive one, the crystallization of writing opposed to the fluid rhythm of spoken language, the monolinguistic opposed to the polyphonic, the discursive opposed to the fixed nature of myth. With a taste inevitably more 'modern' in its mode of expression opposed to the poetic archaism of the dialogue, the commentary unloads a weight of meanings on a fabric woven of expressivity and sound. And, finally, the commentary plays a paradigmatic role, by bringing every moment of the duality within the film to the surface, beginning with the dialogue which, as soon as it stops being the point of a contradiction (Sicilian/Italian), becomes the scene of an opposition: between inside and out; between someone who speaks and someone who is spoken; between the descent towards low culture and its transfiguration, by means of style, into high culture; between the radical political act of opposition and the act, just as radical, of aesthetic enchantment; between the decline in the world represented and its detached contemplation; between the rigorous assumption of what is 'real' and its extreme artifice.

14 Micciché, *Visconti e il neorealismo*, 177ff.

In short, richness of material opposed to richness of form, an extreme realistic vocation in dialectical conflict with an extreme formalist one.

4 *The Leopard*: settings

With Visconti, the setting of a story is the story. (**Marco Ferreri**)[1]

Fifteen years after *La terra trema*, Visconti had set another film in Sicily, *Il Gattopardo/The Leopard* (1963). In this film he shifted the point of view from the lower class and current events of *La terra trema* to the nobility, and the great historical events of the *Risorgimento*. *Il Gattopardo* is based on a novel of the same name by the Sicilian writer Giovanni Tomasi di Lampedusa. The novel narrates the story of Prince Fabrizio di Salina and his family, set against the background of the exploits of the Mille, led by Giuseppe Garibaldi. It began with the landing of Italian revolutionaries, the so-called *camicie rosse* (red shirts) in Sicily in May 1860, and ended in the Campania region in the autumn of the same year with the defeat of the Bourbons and the annexation of southern Italy to the kingdom of Savoy in the North, resulting in the unification of Italy, with the exception of the north-east still under Austrian control.

In 1954, nearly ten years before *Il Gattopardo*, Visconti

---

1 'Visconti created settings essential for the stories he told. None of Visconti's settings is attached, pasted to the story, nor do you feel that it is set design. The setting of a story is the story in Visconti, while the setting of many films is, instead, the setting in which the story takes place.' Maurizio Grande (ed.), *Marco Ferreri: Chiedo Asilo*, Feltrinelli: Milan, 1980, 139.

made *Senso*, set during the third war of independence against Austria, fought in 1866 in the regions of the Veneto, Trentino and Friuli. The nineteenth century and the *Risorgimento* were linked to pictorial naturalism, the melodramas of Giuseppe Verdi and the democratic traditions of Italian culture, crucial elements in Visconti's own formation. This tradition was still strong after World War II, when the Italian Resistance was regarded as a second 'Risorgimento'.

Il Gattopardo narrates the epic of the *Risorgimento* through the disenchanted eyes of Don Fabrizio. At the beginning of the film he is within his sumptuous villa during the 'rosary' ceremony presided over by Father Pirrone in the presence of the entire family: Donna Stella, his eldest sons, Paolo and Francesco Paolo, the youngest son, his daughters Concetta, Caterina, Carolina and Rosalia. The ceremony is interrupted by news of the landing of Garibaldi's troops in Marsala and by the discovery of a dead soldier in the garden of the villa. That same night the Prince goes to Palermo to visit a prostitute, accompanied on the journey by Father Pirrone. The next day, Count Tancredi, the Prince's nephew, tells his uncle that he is about to join Garibaldi's men to fight against the Bourbon king, Franceschiello. Before leaving, Tancredi says goodbye to his cousin, Concetta, who is secretly in love with him. In the Prince's study, Father Pirrone insists that Don Fabrizio confess his sins of the evening before. But the Prince is unapologetic, preferring to reflect on the political situation in Sicily and of the nobility threatened by the growing power of the bourgeoisie and its increasing wealth. Meanwhile, the battle between Garibaldi's men and the Bourbon soldiers is taking place. On Garibaldi's side are, among others, Tancredi and Count Cavriaghi, who Tancredi will later introduce to his uncle's villa, along with a Tuscan Garibaldini general. Despite the war, Don Fabrizio's family sets out on a journey to their holiday palazzo. Their caravan of carriages, escorted by Tancredi, encounters a roadblock by Garibaldini soldiers, which they manage to pass though with some difficulty aided by the good offices of Tancredi. They stop at an inn for the night. The next day, after a picnic in the country, the family reaches the town of Donnafugata, where it is greeted jubilantly by the townspeople and the mayor, Don Calogero Sedara. The family then goes to the cathedral for a Te Deum to give thanks. That evening, Don Calogero is invited to dinner along with his daughter, the beautiful Angelica, with whom Tancredi falls in love. Later on there is a popular vote in the town in favour of the annexation of Sicily to the Kingdom of Savoy. The Prince votes for the Piemontese family, against the Bourbons.

One day, while out hunting with Don Ciccio Tumeo, the church organist, Don Fabrizio comments on the results of the election and asks him for information about Don Calogero's family. He asks Don Calogero for Angelica's hand in marriage on behalf of Tancredi, causing his wife, Donna Stella, to burst into tears, since she wants Tancredi to marry their own daughter, Concetta.

Tancredi, after Garibaldi's army has been disbanded, joins the official army of the King of Savoy, who has become the King of Italy. He returns to his uncle's country villa together with the Tuscan general and Count Cavriaghi, who courts Concetta. Angelica and Tancredi take refuge in an abandoned wing of the villa to flirt with each other. Meanwhile, Cavalier Aymone Chevalley de Monterzuolo comes to Donnafugata to speak with the Prince. After a game of cards, the two retire to the Prince's study, where Chevalley asks Don Fabrizio to become a senator in the new Italian government. The Prince refuses, explaining his philosophy regarding the change from the old political order to the new, the decadence of the nobility and the sensuality of the Sicilian attachment to death.

The remainder of the film takes place in Palermo, in the palace of Prince Ponteleone, where a lavish ball takes place. The Salina family, Tancredi, Angelica and Don Calogero attend the ball. In the labyrinth of rooms and halls filled with precious objects, there is talk of the new political order and the definitive end of the Garibaldi revolution, the emergence of 'transformism' among the new political leaders (cynically stated by Tancredi in one of the early scenes of the film: 'If we want everything to remain as it is, then everything has to change'). Set beside the celebration of the beauty and vitality of Angelica is the pain of Concetta and the Prince's inescapable sense of death. Once the ball comes to an end, the Prince wanders off alone just before dawn into the dark alleys of Palermo.

Objects and characters

The set design of *Il Gattopardo* is not the frame or background of the action, but its foreground, on which the story is inscribed.

The narrative of the film is embedded in externals, in a dazzling world of appearances. The museum-like proliferation of period objects has the look of a sentimental, almost private catalogue; objects become states of mind, tremors from a faded world. The power of its forms correspond to the force of its spirit both objects of nostalgia, at once painful and sensual.

Beauty is conveyed from decor to bodies and from bodies to decor, like the feeling of decadence and death that flows from the chipped statues in the garden of Villa Salina to the petrified, aristocratic profiles looking like funerary statues in the famous Te Deum scene in Donnafugata. The world Visconti evokes is a lost one, in which things have become emanations of character and character emanations of things. The characters, outlined as elements of the set, tend not to stand out from the background, but are almost confounded with it. When characters appear in the foreground, they betray their nature as precious objects: the little fold between Angelica's eyes, like the curling of her lips, have the quality of architectonic moulding engraved by a sculptor's scalpel. Concetta, in her modesty, has the reserved stillness of a pictorial pose. The figure of the Prince recalls heroic statuary of mythological characters whose impressiveness is fused with that of his palaces, with the frescoes that celebrate the glory of his House, and the landscape enclosed by his properties. Don Calogero's small stature, emphasized from his first appearance, evokes the small, vulgar world of parvenus to which he belongs.

Visconti, in creating his characters, often resorted to a stylization of external traits used to mirror inner ones. First and foremost, he worked on shaping appearances, giving characters the same polished unyielding nature as objects have and thereby establishing an accord between men and things. The ideological focus of the film regarding the relation between the nobility and the bourgeoisie, and the old and the new, was filtered through this osmosis of objects and persons. While the gracefulness of princely homes coincided with that of those who lived in them, according to whom 'a palace, all of whose rooms one knows, is not worthy of being inhabited',[2] Don Calogero's formal dress in tails, his electoral office, with its portraits of Vittorio Emanuele and of Garibaldi hung side by side, in clashing frames, irredeemably expressed the crudity, both material and spiritual, of the *nouveau riche*. It suggested that the taste for beauty was a natural aspect of class privilege. It also suggested that things were corrupted by money, reducing them to exchange value. The natural aristocratic pleasure in beauty is contrasted to Don Calogero's monetary calculations when looking at the patrician decor in the ball scene. Tancredi's elegance and fascination instead come, as the Prince says, from squandering the patrimony of his ancestors.

Visconti's closeness to the artistocratic culture of his characters is evident even in his preparation of the film that is completely imitative with respect to the world he stages. With aristocratic ease, for example, he deals with the ceiling frescoes in the Salina palace in only two brief shots, two hundred square metres of depiction, painted in a fortnight by twenty painters based on indications in Lampedusa's novel. At times, Visconti is more subtle: in the final sequence, the Prince was dressed as if he were Giuseppe Verdi in a famous

---

2 This phrase, attributed to the Prince, is referred by Tancredi to Cavriaghi in the scene of the uninhabited rooms.

8 *Il Gattopardo.* The picnic lunch

9 *Il Gattopardo.* Tancredi (Alain Delon) and Angelica (Claudia
     Cardinale) in the empty rooms

painting by Giovanni Boldini, but Visconti avoided showing it in close-up with all its details, so that the similarity or,
better, the citation was only visible in photographs taken on
the set. Far from showing the huge amount of material and
intellectual labour that went into the film, Visconti tended
almost to repress it, dwelling on it only for an instant. He
reduced any detailed vision to a minimum, confounding the
precious singularity of objects and decor in the exuberance
of a mosaic. The frequent overhead or medium shots that
introduce settings serve more to weave objects and characters together in a single impression rather than to flaunt the
sumptuousness of the decor.

Refusing ostentation as typical of the world of *parvenus*,
Visconti almost made a fetish of his cult of the nobility in his
concern for authentic objects borrowed either from antique
shops or directly from the Lanza di Mazzarino family, heirs

10 *Il Gattopardo*. The Prince of Salina (Burt Lancaster) in front of the mirror

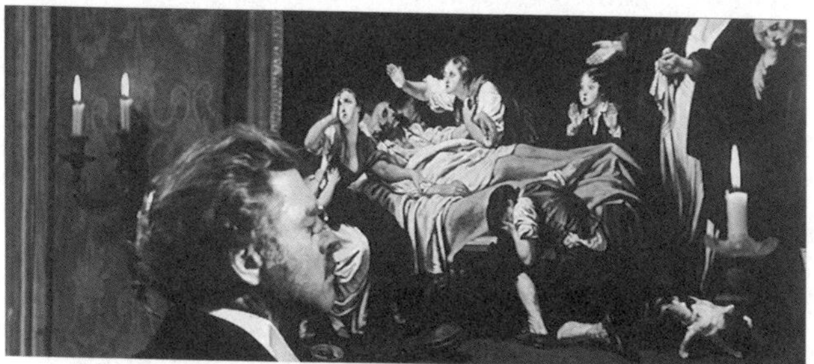

11 *Il Gattopardo*. The Prince of Salina looks at the Jean-Baptiste Greuze painting *The Death of the Just Man*.

of the Lampedusas. His intention was to evoke a seductive authenticity for objects still endowed with an aura by their historical, material existence. It was in contrast to their practical 'exchange value' for the new bourgeoisie in the film and more generally, for the cinema, with its aesthetic of plausibility, verisimilitude, of reproduction 'in the manner of', of the sketching in of a style instead of being the style of a sketch. Visconti opposed, ideologically and emotionally, the plausible for the real, the copy for the original. He was untroubled by the fact that on screen such distinctions would be lost on the spectator. The same spectator, on the other hand, is excluded *a priori* from an entirely other series of rituals involved in the design and sensual aspect of scenes which were of concern to the set only, such as the silk shirts in the Prince's drawers that the camera would never frame and the authentic perfume bottles in the purses of the women at the ball that the camera would never see. Between means and ends, the customary rites of the scene and the simulacra that appear, a vertigo of truth is unleashed from which the spectator is necessarily excluded. This vertigo is entirely consumed on the set, which is experienced as the living space of representation, more theatrical than filmic. Its charm is the lengthy sequence of the ball filmed in Palazzo Gangi in Palermo, for example, by what might be called a documentary technique. It consisted of the use of several cameras situated at different points to capture an uninterrupted performance as if the performance was independent of the filming. The sequence was both functional and seemingly autonomous. Visconti's obsession for authenticity was played out in the gap between what occurred on the set and what was portrayed on the screen.

The true and the false

There were two centres around which the set design of *Il Gattopardo* revolved. One was Visconti's legendary taste for the real as opposed to facsimiles of it. The other, no less fundamental, was the excessiveness of his *mise en scène*. Visconti moved between naturalist extremism and anti-naturalist manipulation. Both the medlar tree in *La terra trema* and the Donnafugata villa, for example, obeyed the same principle of construction. They were an assemblage of real pieces (already existing, not recreated), structured into a fictitious, purely cinematographic unity. In *La terra trema*, instead of reconstructing 'in the manner of', on the basis of a natural model, Visconti assembled real fragments, combining together three different houses in Aci Trezza into one as the house by the medlar tree. He conceived Mara's window as a threshold opening onto two physically non-contiguous spaces that the screen concealed, but that presented itself as an ideal unity, though composed of unrelated material. Similarly, the interiors of Donnafugata did not belong to the Ciminna villa, which represented the Prince's family's summer home in the film, but to Palazzo Chigi in Ariccia, near Rome, while its uninhabited attic was a collage of four attics belonging to four different buildings in Rome and in the surrounding area.

Rather than eliminating the *mise en scène* in favour of an imitative duplication, Visconti strengthened it in the name of the authenticity of the materials used to construct it. He produced the false, the fictitious space of the screen, by putting into play real space. The only setting in *Il Gattopardo* granted an exclusively filmic existence was the Prince's observatory recreated on a site that offered a panoramic view of the Palermo countryside. But, in this case, the creation of the false served both realistic and poetic ends: to show, if only in a few shots, the actual landscape that could be seen through the window as described in the Lampedusa novel. Visconti, as he had done fifteen years earlier in *La terra trema*, used a narrative text as one of the materials of his *mise en scène* giving an equal presence to it as to reality (the locations and Sicilian villas), as he used period objects such as recreated costumes with the addition of original accessories. Such material was carefully prepared. Their source could be a cultural or artistic tradition or, as in *Il Gattopardo*, a literary text, and sometimes all of these.

The choice of settings in the film was governed by finding sites that closely corresponded as much as possible to Lampedusa's descriptions and of following, almost literally, the indications in the novel to such an extent that Visconti remade certain locations. The Boscogrande villa, for example, was subjected to an operation that went beyond simple restoration. Crews of painters worked on the interiors as if they were actual set designs, restoring what was old and creating anew what was described in the novel. Visconti treated real places as if they were set designs and imagined scenic recreations as if they were real places. He had worked on this interweaving of reality and reconstruction, blurring the distinction, since his neorealist period. His stubborn devotion to reality was directly proportional to the extraordinary power of his *mise en scène*. Exactly as in *La terra trema*, a transfigured realism was formed in *Il Gattopardo* by the intersection of two connected, apparently opposed forces: that of the historical, determining the choice of what was real on the set, and reality staged as true in a 'truer than true' falsity.

This dualism of Visconti's inspiration was in fact a single poetic method evident in his films and his theatre work. Visconti began as a set designer in 1936 and often signed the scenery of his own productions in lyric opera and theatre. *Senso* and *Il Gattopardo*, both films in costume, seemed to refer more to Visconti's theatre than to the films that were in contemporary settings. The extreme care he lavished on visual representation, on objects and movements on stage and the expressive use of lighting and colour, distinguish the uninterrupted course he pursued between reality and formalization, an obsessive taste for the real on the one hand, and a love for artifice and a theatrical *mise en scène* on the other. The 'Renaissance-D'Annunzio-like aestheticism', as his style was described,[3] placed Visconti within the great stage tradition of lyric opera, from which, early in the second decade of the twentieth century, Italian history films derived. Without suggesting a direct line between Pastrone's *Cabiria* (1914) and *Il Gattopardo*, it is difficult not to notice that, behind each of them, aside from an aesthetic of the epic spectacle, there is the great scenic tradition of nineteenth-century melodrama, its scrupulous realistic care for detail and the grandiloquence of the whole that characterize, for example, the set designs, especially for Verdi, by Carlo Ferrario at La Scala, from which Visconti took the original scenery for his *Duca d'Alba* by Donizetti in 1959. Visconti's use of actors and the extraordinary care given to their direction brought his experience in the cinema much closer to his theatre. Visconti's actor was always a professional, asked not to be content with mere recitation but instead to enter the character completely. *La terra*

3 Ferruccio Marotti, 'Le regie drammatiche di Visconti', in Mario Sperenzi (ed.), *L'opera di Luchino Visconti*, Fiesole: Atti del Convegno di studi, 27–29 June 1966, 201.

trema was the exception. It both confirmed Visconti's poetics and overturned the terms of it: non-professionals were asked, in this case, to impersonate themselves.

Aside from the *La terra trema*, Visconti did not treat the actors in the same way as he did settings. In *Il Gattopardo*, he juxtaposed his concern for authentic detail to a 'truth' of the characters achieved by acting and dubbing that gave a fictitious unity to the Babel of the film. The rules of the international spectacle film required an American to play the role of a Sicilian. Visconti, who had wanted Laurence Olivier for the part of the Prince, had no problems, however, with a French actor like Alain Delon interpreting Tancredi, even though Visconti was to fill the ballroom of Palazzo Gangi with genuine aristocrats, and when he had to choose the extras for the battle of Palermo he sought physical types from northern Italy to play Garibaldi's soldiers and southern, short and dark types for the Bourbon soldiers. At every level of *Il Gattopardo* there was a split between an extreme naturalism and its negation in staging and acting, which taken together was organized to create a convincing impression of reality.

Painting and pictorial effects

The 'spectacle of wealth' and splendour recreated in *Il Gattopardo* with the remnants of a vanished reality is similar to the 'spectacle of poverty' created in *La terra trema* on the basis of a remote reality suspended in time. 'Ntoni's rags are no less 'precious' than Angelica's costly gowns or those of the Princess, just as the bare, crumbling walls in the houses in Aci Trezza are not figuratively and expressively less 'powerful' than the over-decorated walls of the villas of the nobility. If, in *La terra trema*, reality pretends to be art, in *Il Gattopardo* art pretends to be reality. In the earlier film, Visconti tended to frame reality within a fixed context, while in the later film he sought to bring a past to life. In fact, it is the late nineteenth-century, romantic and, above all, realistic artistic culture that provides the figurative basis for the film.

Paintings among paintings, the images of *Il Gattopardo* belong to the same world as the one represented in the paintings crowding the walls, and are similarly appreciated. Visconti gives us merely passing glimpses of these, pausing only in rare instances – for example, on the gouaches of the estates of the house of Salina in the Prince's study in Donnafugata, the large oil painting in front of which Angelica lingers in the sequence of the empty rooms and *The Death of the Just Man* by Jean-Baptiste Greuze that the Prince contemplates in a sequence set apart during the ball. This painting is the only one with narrative force in the film. It derives, like the others, from the pages of Lampedusa's novel, used to evocative and symbolic effect. *The Death of the Just Man* has a function entrusted to mirrors elsewhere in the film. It is a fundamental element of the decor, but also an accessory 'essential to a world dominated by the visible, by representation, by *fêtes* and theatre'.[4] The mirror doubles and tempers by its reflections, conveying a sense at once striking and vain. Greuze's painting has a feeling of forms peeling away like skin. The Prince contemplates in it his own death.

Much has been said about the pictorial sources of *Il Gattopardo*. The School of the Macchiaioli has been particularly cited, with reference to *Alms* by Silvestro Lega (1864), *Lady in the Garden* by Vito D'Ancona (1861–62), *Fishmonger in Lerici* by Telemaco Signorini (1860), *The Spinner* by Vincenzo Cabianca (1862) and *Garibaldi in Capua* by Giovanni Fattori (1860–62). Other paintings of the same genre and from the same years might also be included, but only in one case, that of Fattori, does it admit to a direct citation: the large door that opens the sequence of the battle between Garibaldi's troops and the Bourbons in the streets of Palermo, especially rebuilt by Visconti in St Euno Square, where the battle had actually taken place. It visibly recalls the Fattori painting, like Visconti's images, crowded with smoke and red shirts. Compared to the scarcity of explicit references, there is a profound cultural

4 Youssef Ishaghpour, *Visconti: le sens et l'image*, Paris: Editions de la Différence, 1984, 8.

and emotional attachment to the figurative world of the nineteenth century, one that formed Visconti's sensibilities and taste. It is a highly composite nineteenth century. Beside the Macchiaioli is the great European realist tradition, the minor *verismo* of the Italian regionalists, and also academic courtly painting. The perfectly dressed characters in *Il Gattopardo* are more reminiscent of Franz Xavier Winterhalter's portraits of the nobility, characterized by an almost photographic clarity and display of costume, than the bourgeois paintings of the Macchiaioli and the French Realists. Visconti's figurative culture in the film is at the threshold of the great Impressionist revolution, while looking back to the theatricality that provides the frame for reality and historical representations typical of much of nineteenth-century painting.

There are many shots in *Il Gattopardo* that create a painterly effect by their composition and lighting, though these are not direct citations of any one painting. As with his depiction of decor, Visconti tends to conceal the difficult work that went into the preparation of each image. The camera's focus is never as fixed and insistent as to be painterly, but instead offers momentary painterly effects as if in passing. Apart from the dead soldier in the garden reminiscent of Böcklin, and perhaps also Courbet, by its surrounding greenery and the sensuality of the soldier's position, and aside too from the *déjeuner sur l'herbe* sequence with its traces of Renoir, Courbet, Manet and of Visconti's memories, the scene in long shot of the leave-taking by Tancredi about to join the Garibaldini, more than vaguely echoing Lega, is strongly atmospheric. The extreme lighting makes objects and figures lose sharpness and become rarefied, while behind them a romantic landscape of palm trees and parched soil seems as if it is a painted background rather than actual nature.

When Tancredi comes to visit the villa with his *Garibaldini*, the characters in the Salina villa are positioned as if on stage or as in a family portrait. The family portrait was a form favoured by Visconti and present in *La terra trema* and *Rocco e i suoi fratelli*, the first two chapters of a hypothetical trilogy on the South brought to completion by *Il Gattopardo*.

In the first hunting scene, proceeding from long shots of the landscape to medium shots of the Prince and Don Ciccio, the images make a figurative leap. The hare hanging from a branch, the hat, the cartridge belt and the rifles leaning against the tree seem staged, as for a study from 'real life'. Wandering through the Donnafugata villa, Tancredi and Angelica encounter not only the perspectival vanishing point of the rooms, but a meticulous rendering of the dust and cobwebs. Against the paintings that have been taken down from the bare walls is the *painterly effect* of the rooms, in particular the small room above the stairway with its perfect composition of the disorder and 'accidental' piles of books, paintings, shutters and cobwebs that seem without depth and are exclusively pictorial, enhanced by diffused lighting that gives to everything a surface effect.

The episode of the stopover at the inn during the journey to Donnafugata is exemplary for the pictorial use of lighting and for its staging. Tancredi is sleeping, lying on some straw in semi-darkness. The camera, in a sequence shot, detaches itself from him in a slow pan that little by little frames dishes and furniture, copper utensils and bread baskets painted almost as still-lives, half consumed by the dark and lined with splashes of light. The camera finally pauses briefly on a medium shot of Father Pirrone at a table with other custom-ers. Behind him, while the camera moves in a forward track, another table of men becomes visible, like forms of colour and light that reverberate in the white of their shirts. To the side is a coat rack full of perfectly arranged dark clothes and hats, modelled by luminous reflections that seem like brush-strokes. It is followed by another medium close-up of Father Pirrone and then a medium shot, broader than the previous one, but with an even more marked compositional order, even if the setting is the same. A wall divides the shot in two, allowing a glimpse of the men at the table in the background and a figure slumped on a chair, perhaps asleep, in a close shot to the right. The next shot begins with another slow pan along the tables, slowly revealing men posing as in a painting. For example, the man in front of a candle with his hand on his cheek is like many of Courbet's subjects and especially the self-portrait of the painter in the placid half- light in *Un après-diner à Ornans* (1849). The next shot, in another room of the tavern, continues the chromatic spell of browns, ochres and yellows, which not even the theatricality of its composition disturbs. Against the background of a wall covered in light and shadow, as if a counterpoint to the first interior shot, is another figure, posed, lying on a bench. And in the next shots of the room where the princes are sleeping, the lighting and composition are evident: perfectly hung clothes, flickering whites in the semi-darkness, the basic colours of brown, ochre and yellow.

This group of short sequences brings together a Realist tradition and nineteenth-century genre painting exemplified by Domenico Induno's descriptive, anecdotal realism, with its theatrical arrangement and the effects of light on small scenes of popular life. The crowing of the rooster off screen confirms the rusticity and sketchiness that Visconti exhibits in his picturing of popular scenes and settings. Generally relegated to the background and seen through the eyes of the nobility, ordinary people rarely appear in *Il Gattopardo* save as extras in the choreographed melodramatic scene of the battle of Palermo or as weak, ideological spokesmen at the close of the roadblock scene or as strongly stylized figures in the scenes of the poor of Palermo and in the alleyways of Donnafugata. Just before the Prince's visit to Mariannina at night is a scene of ordinary people, theatrically lit, that evokes both a film studio and a painting. The same effect is evident in the final sequence of the film in a small town square that, though real, seems constructed. The walls are in ruins, the edge of light coming from the humble house of the dying man, the laundry hanging from the windows, everything composed and staged. The rapid sketches of the life of the people in the streets of Donnafugata recall paintings of La Spezia by Telemaco Signorini. They have a vague folkloric aspect particularly evident in the scene of the alley crossed by the Prince, Chevalley and Don Ciccio at dawn, with the woman on the street feeding the child, another, beyond the open door, rocking her baby and the old lady with the donkey. These are all figures of a descriptive realism directly related to the dominant aesthetic of nineteenth-century painting.

This presence of 'the popular' is in other brief and unimportant shots that function as strategically placed intervals – for example, the peasants watching the gentle folk in the picnic scene in the country, seemingly posed as if in a painting or the peasants hoeing the fields moving their tools almost rhythmically in a brief shot after which, in a cross-fade, the ball scene begins, announced by the music. And finally there is the scene of the plebiscite in which Visconti expressed his sarcasm towards the new bourgeoisie by imitating the folklore of illustrated postcards, for example, of the children, figures of local colour, singing 'Bella Gigogin'.

The drama of light and shadow

The aristocratic interiors are almost always in half-light, illuminated by an imitation of candlelight, causing the white of clothes and decor to flicker. The vast, bare space of the Sicilian landscape contrasts with this world closed within its own richness, wrapped in heavy curtains, suffering from *horror vacui*, seeking to extend itself with perspectival vanishing points in its rooms and with a multitude of mirrors. The luminosity of the countryside is rendered by the warm tones of yellow in the images that temper the sharpness of detail and accentuate the sensation of a monochrome desert that absorbs everything. Outdoors, even the colour of clothes merge with those of nature, and none stand out as if bathed in the atmosphere. The outdoor scenes in *Il Gattopardo* recall the Macchiaioli in their painting of light, recalling certain bare, sunny expanses of land in works by Borrani, Sernesi, Abbati and Costa.

From the first sequence onwards, Visconti stages a contrast between indoors and out as a 'dramatic' one of colour and tone. The bright sunshine of the Sicilian landscape filters through the open windows into the sumptuous interiors of the aristocratic homes in half-light. Shots are framed as if an abyss directed towards a vanishing point of light. Wind billows in the curtains to suggest the breath of History pressing in on the closed world of the nobility. It is only a brief impression, confirmed with the discovery of the dead soldier in the garden of the villa. The impression quickly disappears as the film moves forward.

The landscape in the sequence of the trip to Donnafugata and in the hunting scenes is immobile, indifferent to History. The long and high shots emphasize the epic and solemn opening of the film, at times accentuated by music, and at others by the tolling of bells off screen. A luminous and violent landscape of the soul or an eternal landscape of the gods, Sicily in *Il Gattopardo* is a 'mysterious island' as it is in *La terra trema*. The extent of the land, scorched and monumental, takes the place of Homeric shores furrowed by breakers, evoking a stark, mythical geography as in a Western, which Visconti already had in mind before shooting *La terra trema* when he sent his notes 'for a documentary to be shot in Sicily' to Forges Davanzati.[5]

The direct spokesman of Visconti's feeling about nature is the Prince who, from the window of his observatory, looks out at the landscape and says to Father Pirrone: 'Look how beautiful it is. How many Vittorio Emanueles it would take to transform this magic potion that flows to us every day.' Later 'apparitions' of nature are always linked to the Prince, as he had ideally seen them. It is also the Prince's task to translate feelings into thoughts. The idea of being Sicilian that he presents to Chevalley, as if coming directly from *decadentismo*, invests the landscape with a blend of sensuality, violence

---

5 The document, dated 'Ischia, September 9, 1947', is reprinted in Lino Micciché (ed.), 'Verso *La terra trema*', *La terra trema di Luchino Visconti. Analisi di un capolavoro*, Turin: Associazione Philip Morris–Progetto Cinema–Centro Sperimentale de Cinematografia–Lindau, 1993, 41–42.

and the desire for death typical of the island. Visconti brings together within a single poetic centre the character of the Prince with his sensuous funerary feelings, the beauty of nature and the world of the nobility, expressed by contrasts of colour, blinding light and reflective shadows. The magnificence of a vanishing class can only be compared to the splendour of a landscape, equally immeasurable, grandiose and monumental. And, only because of its 'natural' force, its sexual, almost savage charge, can the beauty of Angelica who comes from a family of *nouveau riche*, be inserted into this system of elective affinities as a reverberation that warms the spirit and the senses.

Il Gattopardo is a drama about a nature that resists history and about a history that is dying. The two worlds – one of eternal immobility, the other of bright, dying reflections – are united by sensual beauty. It is the beauty of the beginning and of the end.

The film opens on the blinding light of nature and aristocratic grace. It concludes on the extinction of reflections, on poverty and death in the darkness of a night changing colour. The circle closes with the light seeking shadows and shadows suspending light.

5 *Vaghe stelle dell' Orsa ...*: remembrances

Vaghe stelle dell'Orsa, io non credea
Tornare ancora per uso a contemplarvi
Sul paterno giardino scintillanti,
E ragionar con voi dalle finestre
Di questo albergo ove abitai fanciullo,
E delle gioie mie vidi la fine.

(Dim stars of the Ursa, I did not think
I would return, as I used
To see you twinkling over father's garden,
And from the window of this house
Where I lived as a child,
And saw the end of my delights.) (**Giacomo Leopardi**)

These verses, which every Italian child once learned in school, are the opening lines of *Le ricordanze/Recollections*, written by Leopardi in around 1830. Citing from the poem as the title of his film, Visconti introduced and commented on the journey to the past and to memory that he was about to undertake with his characters. The phrase 'Vaghe stelle dell'Orsa' entered directly into the narrative of the film as the title of the autobiographical novel of the character, Gianni. The reference to Leopardi was lost in the title chosen by the British distributors, *Of a Thousand Delights* that recalled the dramatic play by John Ford, *'Tis a Pity She's a Whore* (staged by Visconti in Paris, in 1963), with the subject of brother/sister incest.

Prior to the credits in *Vaghe stelle dell'Orsa* ... (1965), Sandra, with her American husband, Andrew, bid their friends good-night at their apartment in Geneva. They leave the following morning for Volterra, the Tuscan city of Sandra's childhood. The occasion for the trip is the donation of the family's villa garden to the city as a public park to commemorate Sandra's father, a Jewish intellectual deported and killed by the Nazis at Auschwitz.

The family home, looked after by the housekeeper, Fosca, is like a museum of relics and a labyrinth of secrets. Andrew observes his wife's unease and seeks in vain to understand the difficulties provoked by memories and emotions associated with the house. That same evening of their arrival Sandra encounters her brother Gianni in the 'paternal garden' near the monument to their father. The signs and echoes of their former incestuous relationship slowly and ambiguously emerge. Immediately after, while accompanying Gianni around Volterra, Andrew tries without success to shed some light on his wife's past. Sandra has chosen to stay in the house with her memories. The two men meet Pietro at the bar. Pietro, the farmer's son who was Sandra's first love, is now a doctor.

The next morning, Sandra meets Pietro waiting for her at the Villa Palagione, where her mother is in hospital. She and her brother suspect their mother and her lover, Gilardini, of having caused their father's arrest. Gilardini is a lawyer who became their stepfather. There is a clear reference in the film to classical tragedy, to Sophocles' *Electra* and Aeschylus' *Libation Bearers* in addition to other literary and cultural echoes: Gabriele D'Annunzio, Marcel Proust, Giorgio Bassani, Eugene O'Neill. The trauma of the meeting at Villa Palagione between Sandra and her demented mother is highlighted in three flashbacks. The first two take place in the subsequent sequence in the town hall, where Sandra and her brother sign the papers donating the garden and there come across Gilardini, who administers the property. The third flashback comes later in the story, when Sandra encounters her brother at the cistern.

After the sequence at the town hall, Sandra tells Andrew about her complicity with her brother against their stepfather and about the fake suicide orchestrated by Gianni to avoid being sent off to boarding school. She also tells him about the secret messages that she and her brother exchanged, showing him the places where they used to hide them. One of these is the pendulum clock with the statues of Cupid and Psyche located in their mother's room. Andrew finds Gianni's note arranging to meet with his sister at the cistern. After having lied to her husband about who had written the note, Sandra secretly goes to the meeting with Gianni. Andrew, at the Etruscan Museum in Volterra, has a conversation with Gilardini, who no longer wants to administer his stepchildren's inheritance. Sandra, meanwhile, has left Gianni at the cistern and returned to the house to read her brother's autobiographical novel. That evening Pietro and Gilardini go to the house, having been invited to dinner by Andrew with the intention of clarifying the tense situation full of hatred, suspicion and secrets. Gilardini, clashing with Sandra, accuses the brother and sister of having an incestuous relationship. Andrew assaults Gianni and decides to leave.

Gianni burns the novel to please Sandra and begs her to stay there with him. Faced with his sister's refusal, he threatens suicide.

Two letters appear on the screen in close succession: one from Andrew, who says goodbye to Sandra; the other from Gianni, who has swallowed sleeping pills to commit suicide. Immediately after is the scene of Gianni in his death agony.

The next morning, the inauguration ceremony of the father's monument is held in the garden. The mother is present, accompanied by Gilardini. Meanwhile, Sandra has written Andrew a letter in which she promises to join him. Pietro, together with Fosca, discovers Gianni's body. They seek out Sandra, in the garden where the ceremony is drawing to a close.

Light and shadow

Inserted between two films in colour, *Vaghe stelle dell'Orsa* ... seems to stand out in Visconti's work like the black-and-white reproduction of a lost painting. Because it seems a dream interlude, it recalls *Le notti bianche/White Nights* (1957), also a low-cost film, produced by Franco Cristaldi, and constructed on the character of an actor, in one case Marcello Mastroianni and in the other, Claudia Cardinale. While the black and white of *White Nights* comes after the highly refined chromatic *Senso* (1954), that of *Vaghe stelle* comes after *Il Gattopardo* (1963), another historical fresco in colour, and before the strident use of colour in *Lo straniero/The Stranger* (1967). On closer examination and independent of the issue of colour or not, Visconti's *mise en scène* in these films exhibit the same obsession with lighting. The struggle between the opposing forces in his films of life and death, reality and utopia, nature and history, the new and the old, inside and out, being and nothingness, is subject to contrasts of light and dark, shadows that consume and light that blinds.

In *Il Gattopardo* and *Lo straniero*, the outdoor scenes tend to be monochromatic, bathed in a light that blurs the outlines of things, making them seem almost unreal, both mythic and estranged. Indoor scenes, to the contrary, are in half-light, creating density and the darkness in the second half of *Lo straniero*, where the cell is encroached upon by the blackness of death. In *Vaghe stelle dell'Orsa* ... a pale, diffused illumination characterizes the pre-credit sequence in the apartment in Geneva, where the credits are sharply detached from the main body of the film. The overexposure in the cinematography dominates in the images of the journey on which the title credits are printed. It lends an air of the fantastic to objects and landscapes framed by the camera from the car. That unreal light is cut through by two brief moments in black as the car goes through tunnels. The black has a natural cause but also assumes a symbolic connotation. The journey leads to a change of dimensions. As in films of the fantastic, a dark tunnel can open onto imaginary time and space, a form of passage towards an elsewhere.

Space and time in *Vaghe stelle* are subjected to a process of abstraction and suspension, which tend to become represented as paths of shadow and light. This ambiguity, which Visconti indicated as the dominant theme and final sense of the work, was first evident in the uncertainty of these dimensions, abandoned to the pulsations of black and white or, as Suzanne Liandrat-Guigues writes, to the constant 'sparkling' of matter as it passes into energy.[1]

Once in Volterra, the film almost completely takes place within the old house. A marked whiteness bathes the only two outdoor shots during the day: the sequence of the visit to the mother, and the final ceremony where black by contrast is emphasized and the wide-angle lens increases the anguish of the final shot. Otherwise, inside the house there seems to be endless night. At times Visconti suspends his characters in thick darkness before lights are turned on as they cross the thresholds of uninhabited rooms. The rooms seem to have few links with the outside and assume shape only by internal sources of light, as on a theatre stage. There is a continuous alternation of light and dark, reflections of brightness and falling shadows. Occasionally, an almost unnatural opaque glow seems to come from the outside as when Sandra approaches the closed shutters before joining Gianni at the cistern, when she reads her brother's manuscript in their mother's room touched by reflections from the flames in the fireplace, and when she finally opens the window on the morning of the fourth day, a moment before descending into the garden for the inauguration of her father's monument. In this last image, like a prelude to an act of liberation, as if communication with the outside had sanctioned an end to an agonizing seclusion, is the discovery of Gianni's body shown reflected in a mirror. He is lying on the ground stretched out towards

---

1 Suzanne Liandrat-Guigues, *Les Images du temps dans 'Vaghe stelle dell'Orsa ...' de Luchino Visconti*, Paris: Presses de la Sorbonne Nouvelle, 1995, and 'Lo scintillio in "Vaghe stelle dell'Orsa ..."', in David Bruni and Veronica Pravadelli (eds), *Studi viscontiani*, Venice: Marsilio, 1997, 121–129.

the morning light filtered through partially open curtains. By using alternating montage to orchestrate the sequence in a dramatic counterpoint of indoor and outdoor, Pietro's gesture of covering the body is repeated by Sandra, by contrast, when she unveils the bust of their father. The passage from shadow to daylight is like a succession of the dead, father and son together consecrated by the rabbi's requiem in the only apparently luminous perspective of a future resurrection in which the earth 'shall restore life to the shadows', the same light that radiates in the last shot of the film in lengthening shadows, more evening than morning light.

The other two outdoor sequences are at night: the encounter between brother and sister in the garden, and Andrew and Gianni's visit to Volterra. Visconti's use of light and his set design in both these sequences are expressionist. In the first, the old creaking door leading to the park bangs violently in the wind. Andrew believes he has seen a ghost. Behind the glass of the window Fosca is silhouetted like a disturbing apparition. Her name, Fosca (gloomy, dark), though common in Tuscany, is emblematic. The mysterious atmosphere created is a prelude to a hallucination, a *coup de théâtre*. After reassuring her husband about the absence of ghosts, Sandra crosses the threshold that separates the space in the house devoted to her mother from the garden associated with the memory of her father. The wind suddenly shifts a white cloth that flashes in the dark. The statue of the father covered by a white sheet is ghost-like. Immediately after, Sandra and the camera move towards each other to reveal an embrace beside the veiled bust of her father. What turns out to be a false ghost immediately evokes another. In the following shot, the brother appears behind the iron grill of the gate, his face half-eaten away by the shadow. He is a substitute icon of the father, the incarnation of love for an absent subject. The glow of the sheet immediately turns into that of flesh and the hands of the brother and sister seeking one another in the darkness of night. The symbolic value of the natural elements (the wind and the century-old trees) and those of the set design (the gate, the statue animated by the drapery) join together in the dramatic effect of white as the spectral colour of absence and mourning, juxtaposed to black, the repressed of fear and guilt.

In the sequence of Gianni and Andrew's wanderings among Le Balze (the Ravines) and then along the streets of Volterra, alternating with Sandra's foray into her mother's flat, there is a contrast between wild nature and the ancient silent funereal city as a projection of her inner anxieties. Volterra is a place of ruins and tombs, with the same mortuary destiny as the characters wandering in a temporal vortex. In their pale raincoats blasted by the wind, Gianni and Andrew cross Volterra like ghostly figures who have been flung down into a nowhere of the imagination. While the white of their coats sparkles in the dark, their black silhouettes are projected onto the ruins of the past. Lamps vibrate in the wind, producing bands of wavering light that accompany the two men walking along a deserted street in a long shot from above.

The contrast between light and dark zones becomes extremely stylized in the sequence. The allusiveness of Gianni's character is reduced to formula through the recurrence of shadows inlaid on his flesh. As Gianni speaks, his face enters and exits zones of light, emerging and disappearing. It is a game he plays throughout the film of revealing himself and withdrawing, saying and not saying, between his inability to fully come out into the light and the sensual pleasure of being in shadow. It is emblematic of the romantic and decadent conflict between Eros and Thanatos often stressed by Visconti. Gianni is the expressionist hero out of the kingdom of the shadows and into which he is eventually drawn. His death will take place between the torment of a night passing into a new day accompanied by the ringing of the morning church bells.

Visconti gives the same weight to lighting as he does to the gestures of his characters. Like their stylized poses, at times recalling the diva-like rhetoric of silent film, his lighting gives to space similar allusive and disturbing inflections. As for faces, he paints them in light with the sharpness of expressionism, for example, in the alternating close-ups of Sandra, Gianni and Andrew, each alone in their beds on the first night in Volterra, moving shadows passing over their faces. The use of the zoom in these shots has the same function as the lighting, to intensify rhythms and create significances. The reverse zoom from Gianni's eyes to his face is followed by a forward zoom from Sandra's face to her eyes. The contrasting movement excludes Andrew and traces a direct passionate closeness between brother and sister. The husband is extraneous. He exists indirectly as an effect unable to understand the theatrical play of light and shadow in the spaces occupied now and in the past by the family.

The segregated space of the unconscious

As in ancient castles of Gothic novels, the old family home has a secret wing, the mother's quarters, the pulsating heart of the house, in which mystery thickens and dramas explode. The night Sandra arrives in Volterra, she enters this zone having rid herself of husband and brother. She is looking for herself and for an unresolved truth she will never grasp. Her immersion in the past is visibly a return to the body of her mother and the mother's madness that the house reflects. This descent into the abyss finds its most extreme realization in the sequence at the cistern, a deep, watery place that inevitably evokes the maternal womb. 'This is our house,' Gianni says to his sister, reminding her of their childhood meetings in the dark cavern they used as a refuge. The spiral staircase marks off the passage from the external to the internal world.

It is difficult not to resist the temptation to read into this mythical realm of memories and desires the cinema itself, a place where semblances of consciousness are shaped and projected shadows of things vibrate as in Plato's cave. Here too light produces the fleeting reflection of bodies while the surface of water acts as a screen. Elsewhere in the film mirrors and glass reinforce this precarious sense of appearances doubled, true in all of Visconti's works.

The journey that Sandra has begun in order to lend reality to her terrible ghosts, and perhaps also to serve as an alibi for her troubled conscience, has pushed her into the unsteadiness of the unconscious towards which she feels both attracted and repelled. In the cistern sequence, Visconti organized what psychoanalysts call the mirror stage, the passage from the identification by a child with the body of the mother to the desperate solitude of self-recognition as an individual. Leaving behind the reflection in the water, Sandra escapes that primary indistinctness and abandons the floating image of her brother, an orphan contemplating himself.

The film alludes to a certain fatality in its reproduction of archetypical figures. If, at times, Gianni plays the role of the father in relation to Sandra, to him she plays the absent mother. Visconti continuously lays stress on ties and associations between Sandra and her mother and both take refuge beneath a wide-brimmed hat that recalls Giovanna's mourning hat in *Ossessione* (1943) and repeats the gesture of the black-gloved hand covering their faces.

The first time Sandra bursts into her mother's apartment, she caresses the plaster mould of a hand almost certainly that of her mother, a musician who played César Franck's *Prelude, Chorale and Fugue*, just as Visconti's own mother, Carla Erba, had done in real life. The hand immediately takes on the significance of a fetish to which Visconti would often return. Sandra's hands, as well as those of the other characters, are often lighted as if they were sculpted, giving them expressive plastic force. Not only does Sandra's repeated gesture of passing her fingers over her face as if tormenting and hiding it come to mind, but so too the image of her hands clutching the veiled bust of her father the evening of her arrival in Volterra and which Gianni kisses during their first meeting. There is also Andrew's hand that appears in the background of the shot caressing his wife's nude back and then immediately is withdrawn. It is as if the touch had come from another world, interrupting a hypnotic transference to the past. There are many other examples, including the symbolically strongest detail in the sequence at the cistern when Gianni removes Sandra's wedding ring from her finger. The same image occurs later at the height of the dramatic clash between brother and sister in a close-up of Gianni's hand with the ring on his little finger, grasping Sandra's hand and then moving up her arm.

Visconti combined elements of Palazzo Inghirami in Volterra, where Gabriele D'Annunzio had set his *Forse che sì forse che no/Maybe Yes, Maybe No* (1910), with aspects of Palazzo Viti to create the family home in the film. There are no traces in it of the father's presence. Everything leads back to the mother. The pendulum clock on the chest of drawers depicting Eros and Psyche represents the somewhat puzzling sensual embrace between Sandra and Gianni. It is as if Psyche in the myth cannot decide whom she really loves. Andrew discovers the note from Gianni hidden in the sculptured folds of the ornamental clock inviting his sister to the meeting at the cistern. A forward zoom emphasizes the metaphorical significance of the mythical figures in marble later repeated in the clash between Gianni and Sandra when the camera abandons their clasped bodies embracing in the darkness to focus on the neoclassical pendulum in a lateral track bathed in light. Off screen can be heard the agitated voices of the two and Gianni's appeal to his sister not to leave him, in contrast to the classical myth. The next shot remains focused on the clock, zooming in on it, while the dialogue continues off screen. Finally, Gianni's hand, then his entire body, followed by an upward pan, enters the frame taking medicine from the top dresser drawer that he will use for the suicide threatened a moment earlier.

Thus the 'explanations', as deceptive as they may be, take place in the mother's room. It is there that Gianni's novel of the same title as Visconti's film is read and destroyed and from which the spectator might have hoped for evidential 'proof' of incest, but receives instead only an account of Gianni's desire which he never concealed. The clues are uncertain and vague, true to Leopardi's formulation, as are all other indications in the film.

The mother's quarters are also the stage of the dinner which reunites the characters and represents – a recurrent pattern in Visconti's films – the moment in which differences erupt and allusions are given substance, even if to no avail. In short, the central locations of action end up as if emanating from the body of the mother. The oxymoron of the mother's continuous vacant presence is made manifest as early as the prologue in the music by César Franck which, though diegetically motivated (there is a pianist playing on stage), creates a kind of space–time block reinforced by the forward zoom on Sandra's face turned aside and then seen frontally. She is seen trying to conceal her expression of worry like a sculpted fold revealing her inner torment, as happens often in the film. In conducting his own 'spiritual quiz',[2] Visconti refers back to the mother–daughter encounter at the Villa Palagione to explain the disturbance created by the music. The notes of Franck's music are for the second time played by the mother and belong directly to the diegetic world of the film. In the rest of the film, they will have the function of evoking her by her absence.

Already dispersed, and as if a metaphor of childhood, the mother's presence is made manifest by sound to become a musical motif which breaks through space and causes time to fluctuate. Her actual entrances are like apparitions of a diva marked by neuroses and age. Before selecting Marie Bell for the role, Visconti had considered Francesca Bertini, as well as other Italian stars of the silent period.

In other words, the mother's time is the eternal past lodged in Sandra's memory and in the objects and sepul-chral spaces of the house, the reason her actual presence only partially belongs to the present and appears, rather than in the real progression of events, as an enlargement of memory in Sandra's three flashbacks. These detach the scene of the

2 Visconti, Un *dramma del non essere*, in Pietro Bianchi (ed.), *Vaghe stelle dell'Orsa ...*, Bologna: Cappelli, 1965, 34.

mother–daughter meeting from the objective linear time of the story.

The slippages of time

The course of *Vaghe stelle dell'Orsa* ... moves towards a unity of time, place and action like a *Kammerspiel*.[33] The action, essentially taking place within the palazzo, occurs over four days, from the evening of the first day in Geneva to the morning of the last in Volterra. This progression of events is interrupted by a slippage into the past. Images waver on the threshold between one dimension and the other. As early as the prologue, the past, evoked by the notes of Franck's music, plunges into the present and immobilizes it. That first zoom is accompanied by a fading of surrounding noise as Sandra immediately seems to be swallowed up by a landslide.

The metaphor of a landslide used by Visconti to describe the landscape of Volterra is particularly suited to illustrate the space/time dimensions of the film. The shots of the trip to Italy move the characters not only from one place to another but into the world of their ghosts and phantasies. Once in Volterra a series of clues indicate that passage. Sandra's hair, which in Geneva is cut short in a modern coif, is now long, as it was in her childhood. Her first gesture as soon as she takes possession of the guest room is to let her hair down in front of the mirror, which becomes clouded with time. Visconti shows this slippage of time and place by an evident break in the editing. Less than twenty-four hours have passed since the evening of the party in Geneva and the arrival in Volterra.

The obliteration of time contrasts with the representation of space. These slippages are manifest in intersecting signs between the *mise en scène* and the language of the film. There is, for example, the matter of the arrangement of Sandra's

3 Visconti: 'From the old "kammerspiel" of Mayer and Lupu Pick, it shall have only the relative unity of time and place, the highly colorful dramatic initial idea, an abundance of close-ups, that is, all things which are completely accidental'; Visconti, Un dramma del non essere, 32.

hair different from one scene to the next, the braid wound around her head in Etruscan style in the cistern sequence, and then falling loosely over her shoulders during the reading of the novel in front of the fireplace. Dress also evokes states of mind and the passing of time by changes of style and a play on combinations of black and white.

The circularity of time is reflected in accessories and gestures. The film unfolds as a dense network of correspondences between its figures, their attitudes and looks. The leitmotiv of the white veil, for instance, passes from one character to another. It is the shroud of the dead father, Sandra's fluttering shawl in the first sequence in the garden and, shortly after, used by Gianni to mask his face. It returns in the next scene involving the hand towel, which Gianni passes over his face, and then at the end in Sandra's reflective gesture with the bath towel, echoed by the white handkerchief matched with her dress. Sandra's tears in the last sequence reproduce those at the beginning on the evening of her arrival. Sandra's bare back rhymes with her brother's nude torso. Their relationship, continuously alluded to in words and looks, is also suggested by the sensuality and beauty of their unveiled bodies. Insofar as these contrasts evoke the father and mother, Gilardini and Andrew are linked as extraneous figures.

The dialogue at times expresses both the return to a past and the duplication of symmetries, for example, the conversation between Andrew and Gilardini in the Etruscan museum is a counterpart to the scene involving Gianni outdoors at night. In both cases explanations are partial and ambiguous. Andrew masks his incomprehension by a presumption of knowledge. 'Gianni told me about that', he tells Sandra and 'Sandra told me about that', he replies to Gilardini. Sandra reprimands Andrew for being 'jealous of the wandering shadows' in the house, while later Gianni will accuse her of being afraid 'of the sudden return of a memory, the sound of a voice ... a certain colour'. The suspicions that brother and sister voice about the love affair between their mother and

Gilardini turn back upon their own relation.

The insistent figures of doubling and inversions in roles and situations is also manifest in reverse shots throughout the film, beginning with the drive to Volterra, where the car is framed without respect for narrative continuity. There are frequent jump-cuts, sudden variations of light and abrupt spatial reversals. In addition there are reverse shots that create a mirror effect, with all that it implies. In the dinner sequence, the hall of the mother's apartment, until then framed from a single point of view, is composed of two almost perfectly symmetrical halves like mirror images. In contrast to the lengthy conversation between Sandra and Andrew behind the partially open curtains of the mother's bed, the shot of the death throes of Gianni in the midst of those curtains is from a reverse point of view.

Just when Visconti is stressing the mental character of what is represented, he carefully fills the scene with chronometric instruments that at once deny and reinforce temporal uncertainties; for example, the pendulum clock in the guest room whose ticking is prolonged into the beginning of the sequence at the cistern as to seem outside the diegesis evoking the beating of a heart in turmoil. And there is the tolling of the bell in the tower immersed in the shadows of night that seems to come from another era. In the final sequence, the pealing of bells greets the mournful arrival of day.

In addition to the music of César Franck, which theatrically shares in the superimpositions of time, sound in the film is involved in the same system of echoes that rule the images playing on the double dimension of being on the surface and existing in a depth, as occurs with the clocks throughout the house and the songs from times past heard on the evening of the arrival in Volterra and that seem to mime events and character while also underlining the immobility of remnants from the past, their resistance to time.

The contrast between old and new, represented above all by the figure of Andrew, becomes less marked in the passage from script to filming. What remains, however, is the idea that the modern instruments of capturing reality (Andrew's amateur camera and his statistics) are incapable of understanding the true state of things. The irrelevance of Andrew to the drama unfolding often has a spatial dimension. Visconti places him on thresholds, both spectator and intruder to scenes where he is out of place, pushed to the sidelines. He loses his way in the house and with his wife, as if his relation to both is similar. Visconti's camera zooms less often on Andrew than it does on Gianni and Sandra.

This movement of the lens, which appears for the first time in a systematic and obsessive manner in this film, not only functions to foreshorten views and limit the need to fragment scenes into many shots, but is also the principal instrument for the derealization of time.[4] It is appropriate, therefore, that the zoom is only seldom used on Andrew, who is someone content merely with appearances.

A forward zoom creates a void around the subject. It is the equivalent of an extreme fixed pose, of a high note in opera or a silence extended unnaturally. By such means, a melodramatic emphasis is achieved without hesitation or mediation, a violent gesture that declares the presence of Visconti in the *mise en scène*. On the other hand, a backward zoom, from a close-up on a detail to a wide shot of a scene, sometimes gives the impression that the image issues from the character's point of view. This is the case of the shot that shows Sandra entering her mother's rooms for the first time, where the zoom reveals the space unexpectedly.

The frequency of close-ups, sometimes in a tracking shot, contributes to the suspension of space–time, while jump cuts provide a sense of circularity between past and present and a mirroring of characters. Only once, in the sequence in Geneva, does Visconti use a fade, where it functions as a present prologue to a story in the past. By renouncing from then onwards this classic mark of punctuation to signify the passage of time or separate the true from the imaginary, the

4 Youssef Ishaghpour, *Luchino Visconti: le sens et l'image*, Paris: Editions de la Différence, 1984, 137–138.

present from memories of the past, it permits a constant overlap of various levels of time and reality. To express the circularity of time, the ellipse created by jump cuts does not respect either spatial or temporal continuity. Characters appear topographically, revealed in stages, which results in an unresolved spatial suspension. The mother's room, for example, is not seen in a single comprehensive glance, but in slices, fragments, which prevents the pieces from coming together to form a whole.

Sometimes a false continuity in the dialogue covers over slight spatial and temporal gaps. In fact, Visconti tends almost totally to eliminate a *mise en scène* in transitions between place and seems unconcerned to motivate such changes. Characters suddenly appear on stage, bursting in as Gianni does through a gate or curtain in the sequence of the reading of the novel.

The semi-hidden figure behind drapery, passing through transparent curtains and reflected in the mirrors, is a recurrent motif, not only in *Vaghe stelle* but in all Visconti's films. In this film, it is perfectly in harmony with its fundamental theme of an impossible unveiling.[5] The entire film concerns the vain desire to uncover an enigma, symbolized in the veiled statue of the father. But no truth will emerge from beneath the cover and defence of the characters. Gianni, the only character to attempt to throw off the veil, will atone for it by his suicide.

Shawls and curtains perform the same function as light and shadow, hiding and revealing the labyrinth of the bad conscience of the characters, crushed by the unspeakable weight of suspicion, betrayal, incest and madness. The 'mystery' Visconti says he wants to represent is without resolution and appears, as he himself admits, 'clear from the beginning' and 'obscure at the end, as each time someone undertakes the difficult task of self examination certain

---

5 '... the ambiguity of the real, its intangibility, the resulting defeat of knowledge, belongs to the essential grammar of the film'; Luciano De Giusti, *I film di Luchino Visconti*, Rome: Gremese, 1985, 107.

to have nothing further to learn then finds himself in the anguish of non-being'.[6]

The glimmer of a happy ending, imposed by the producers, that some critics found in Sandra's letter to her husband, is illusory. Gianni's death rekindles the tragic play of responsibility and blame. As a reflection of the father's 'homicide', it drives the story back to its beginning and makes any 'resolution' useless. The fatality of destiny and the past, which Visconti has always staged, is the only clear point in this regressive journey, which leads to nothingness and to death.

In line with the title that reproduces the beginning of Leopardi's *Le ricordanze, Vaghe stelle dell'Orsa* ... recounts the vertigo of the individual seeking to repress the past (reflecting on the fate of Auschwitz, its historical equivalent), and the impossibility of escaping it and, at the same time, rediscovering 'lost time'. In this enquiry 'on the dissolution of the family', 'in the manner of Sophocles',[7] frequently at the centre of his films, Visconti stages the pulse of life and death as obscure natural forces: wind, water, dust, fire and air, the substance of an eternal tragedy that repeats itself.

The film is an archive of memories, filled with objects and symbolic gestures, at the same time depicting Visconti's recollections, existential, artistic and cultural. Critics have made an inventory of the various sources of the film, literary and otherwise. It needs to be said, however, that *Vaghe stelle dell'Orsa* ... is not tied to any text in particular, but to that deposit of material, memory and experiences that constitutes the poetics of Visconti. On the same level as dream, memory is a novelistic evocation of existence and desire, reality and the imaginary. The literary aura of the film, then, is not an ornamental covering but something alive, even if dying, into which the film immerses itself.

6　Visconti, *Un dramma del non essere.*

7　'Visconti: "Se ho plagiato qualcuno si tratta di Sofocle e non di Bassani" [an account of an encounter between the director and the press]', *La Gazzetta del Popolo,* ed. Piero Novelli, 3 September 1965.

6 Pasolini: heaven and earth

Pier Paolo Pasolini was brutally murdered on 2 November 1975, at the age of 53. His life and (above all) his death are now shrouded in myth and the inevitable rhetoric that marks the destinies of 'martyrs'.

Persecuted for his homosexuality, he was forced to leave Friuli, where he had returned during the war. His mother was from Friuli and it was there he wrote his first poems in Friulian dialect. After having been subjected to the first of thirty-three judicial trials that were to mark his life, he moved permanently to Rome with his mother in 1950, where he lived at the periphery, in the *borgate* of the city. Its inhabitants, the sub-proletariat of Rome, became the main subject of his poetry and stories. His beginnings as a writer with the novel *Ragazzi di vita/The Ragazzi* (1955) resulted in a scandal that would accompany his every gesture in the future.

His relationship with the cinema began in the mid-1950s as a scriptwriter. His first film, *Accattone* (1961), was followed by *Mamma Roma* (1962) and then by the short film, *La Ricotta/Cream Cheese* (1963). These constituted his trilogy on the Rome *borgate* represented as a mythical place in which the material and moral poverty of its characters are redeemed by an 'epic religious' point of view. From 1963 he ventured into documentary, experimenting with investigative films, *Comizi d'amore/Love Meetings* (1963), films based on a montage of already existing images, *La rabbia/Rage* (1963) and films in the form of 'notes for a film to be made': *Sopraluoghi in Palestina per il Film* Il Vangelo secondo Matteo/*Looking for Locations in Palestine for the film* The Gospel According to Matthew (1963–65), *Appunti per un film sull'India/Notes for a Film on India* (1967–68), *Appunti per un'Oresteia africana/Notes for an African Orestiade* (1968–73). After *Il Vangelo secondo Matteo* (1964), a portrait of a revolutionary Christ who defies contemporary society and its lack of values, he made *Uccellacci e uccellini* (1966), a definite break from the neorealism of his earlier films. *Uccellacci e uccellini* is characterized by a Marxist commitment and the assumption of the role of 'civic' artist. His metaphysical tales about death, the relationship between life and dreams, and life and representation – *La terra vista dalla luna/*The *Earth as Seen from the Moon* (1967), *Che cosa sono le nuvole?/What are Clouds?* (1968), *La sequenza del fiore di carta/Paper Flower Sequence* (1969) – are from the same period as his theoretical research into the language of film, 'heretical' in relation to the then current structuralist and semiological studies of film. His interest in Greek myth and tragedy dates back to the mid-1960s, in such films as *Edipo re/Oedipus Rex* (1967) and *Medea* (1969). *Porcile/Pigsty* (1969) was instead an adaptation of one of the Pasolini's theatre pieces, while *Teorema* (1968) recounts the visitation of a divine personage who reveals himself to men and women through the 'scandalous' power of sex. *Teorema* appeared as a book and as a film.

Between the late 1960s and the early 1970s, Pasolini further complicated his literary reputation by writing texts of a hybrid and indefinable nature, all intensely experimental. His films, on the contrary, seemed to move in a different direction, that of a return to tradition involving problems of narration. He revisited some of the most important early literary narratives: *Il Decameron/The Decameron* (1971), *I racconti di Canterbury/ The Canterbury Tales* (1972) and *Il fiore delle Mille e una notte/ Arabian Nights* (1974).

Pasolini again surprised critics and the public with his last film, *Salò o le 120 giornate di Sodoma/Salò, or the 120 Days of Sodom* (1975), an extreme work in which sexuality and violence became, as Pasolini stated, cold metaphors of a loathsome consumer society.

Among the various aspects and themes of his activities, this chapter concentrates on a recurrent pattern in his writing and his films, the accord and contrast between heaven and earth. This figurative polarity makes it possible to revisit Pasolini's entire career, his archetypes and the most emblematic signs of his world-view and concept of art.

The scene of origins

Images of heaven and earth, of their closeness and contrast, constitute the scene of origins in Pasolini's poetry; in his 'philosophy', that scene is the natural, primitive one before History and civilization, a sacred scene of birth and death, of the beginning and the end.

In the prologue to *Edipo re*, which is clearly autobiographical, the scene of origins is constructed of various shots from the child's point of view. In the first of these the camera is barely above ground and the little child can only see the legs of his mother and those of the other women trampling the lawn as they bustle about, running, playing, setting a tablecloth on the grass. His point of view is subsequently raised towards the sky in a whirling pan of the sky seen through the lacework of the poplar trees. Finally, his view passes from the sky and the trees back to the grass, where it ends. The epilogue of the film – in which Oedipus, having gone through his tragedy, returns to his birthplace – is perfectly symmetrical to the prologue. The final shot in the film is of the grass on a lawn in Friuli on which Oedipus' eyes as a child had rested and to which he now turns his blind gaze as an adult at the end of his life. Oedipus, though blind, has no need to see because the earlier image is within him. 'Life ends where it begins', says Pasolini, underscoring the sense of circularity in the finale of the film. This cycle is recurrent in his work and, in this case, more explicit than elsewhere, expresses an obsession with a return to origins as the loss of self.

The scene of origins is the hinge on which unstable and agonizing games of history and aesthetics are played out. It is something more than a gilded backdrop in his Friulian poetry or the sullied in his Roman poetry and films. It is the scene that underlies and is prior to all other possible ones – from which one departs and returns – no matter if with nostalgia or a sensual desire for annihilation. It survives, unperturbed, even beyond the self-destruction of Pasolini's nihilist gestures towards the end of his life. The dark rewriting, almost thirty years later, of *La meglio gioventù* (1954) in *La nuova gioventù* (1975),[1] testifies, even if by negation, to the unyielding nature of the scene of origins. It makes possible his own double degradation and allows for the futile closure of the circle in a nothingness shared by the end and the beginning.

The garden

In the Friulian poems from *La meglio gioventù*, heaven and earth constitute a singular Arcadian scene, an idyllic place simultaneously affirmed and negated. Pasolini extolled the communion of the high and low as a sort of indistinctness of origins. The world appeared to him as the emanation of the body of Narcissus (the favourite character of his poems at the time) that contemplates its own dissemination and dismemberment in nature. The body of the poet is dissolved into the colours, smells and shapes of the landscape.

The earth is 'liberated in the sky' and the sky 'rains' and 'laughs' on the young peasant. This communion of heaven

1 Under the title *La meglio gioventù* in 1954 Pasolini published the poems he had written in Friulian between 1941 and 1953, together with their Italian versions. In 1975, he published *La nuova gioventù*, a book divided into two parts: the first part was a faithful reprinting of *La meglio gioventù*; the second was introduced as 'La nuova forma de "La meglio goventù"' ('The New Form of "La meglio gioventù"') and was a rewriting, which he did in 1973–74, of the verses in the first book. The register that Pasolini used this time was that of negation, which necessitated a radical change of the tone, content and feeling that had been guidelines in *La meglio gioventù*.

and earth is represented as the flow of death and life. The dead and the living converse with each other and everything that disappears returns in nature as in bodies. Children have the traits of their fathers and 'time does not move'. It is circular, shaped like an egg, as Pasolini would later write in his poems at the end of the screenplay of *Medea*. The favourite moments of the day are dawn and evening, moments of passage, of the opening and closing of the circle.

Friuli, what the poet calls 'a region of the spirit', regressive and maternal, foreshadows the Promised Land, the myth of an evergreen season, of spring as eternal youth. But, as always occurs with Pasolini's forms, the myth is divided, separated, disharmonic. The song of Paradise is, from the very beginning, the song of a Paradise lost, ready to be transformed into the song of nothingness and its mystery. Spring wears a funereal mask, everything that is vital reeks of death, of eternal passages. And the more the vortex of this original mortal emptiness appears, the more the poet's floral mannerism, as Franco Fortini defined it, expands into a description of the leaves and petals in the Friulian Garden. The predominant colour is light blue; the favourite flower, the violet; the favourite month, April; and the favourite holiday, Easter. The air always resounds, pierced by the ringing of bells. Smells are intoxicating ('Friuli is a fragrance', Pasolini later said). Light blindingly rains down on bodies and the earth. In the Italian version of the poem, *A Rosari*, he says: 'On the earth flesh is heavy, in the sky it is made of light. Do not lower your eyes, poor youth, if a shadow weighs in the womb/Laugh, agile youth, feeling the dark warm earth and the cool clear sky in your body'.

This celestial blue light, that becomes fragrant and full of sounds as it spreads its rays over bodies, is, at the same time, and fatally, a distant radiance. Pasolini simultaneously glorifies and denies communion between low and high, sombre and bright, darkness and light. The sky is near, having hurled itself into the breast of the youth from Friuli, and also irredeemably distant, closed in the eternal and immobile silence

12 *Accattone*. The vision of Paradise in the dream sequence

13 *Uccellacci e uccellini*. Street

14 *Edipo re*. The Mother (Silvana Mangano)

15 *Che cosa sono le nuvole?*

16 *Medea*. Title

17 *Teorema*. Mount Etna

of its own blue as if ecstatic over nothing, over a void. The light-hued sky changed colour into a 'dark fire', and the kingdom of a distant father to whom the youthful mother and her child turned on Palm Sunday: 'vignín tal sèil par no vivi pí / veniamo nel cielo per non vivere più' (We enter the sky to stop living).

The waste land

In the move from the pastoral images of Friuli to the slums of Rome, the scene of origins does not change so much as it undergoes the first of many 'transformations' (*rifacimenti*).[2] The funereal paradise of Friuli becomes the heavenly hell of the slums. The young peasant boys, fallen like angels 'from the heart of the sky', are replaced by slum youths with dirty faces from the underworld, walking in mud, dust, garbage amidst an overpowering stench. The Garden is displaced by a land abandoned by God, a Waste Land, in a descent under the sign of the loss of the heavenly and a perpetual dream of it.

The idea of hell – and of death in general – is linked in *Accattone* to the earth tormented by the blinding white light of the sun like a deathly echo. Bodies consumed by light, unable to rise up from the ground, are conflated with mud. Accattone sinks his face into the dark sand, then raises it. It seems an almost demoniac death mask. The dead bodies of the Neapolitans are covered with dirt. A desert of dirt is the image that Accattone has of his own death in the dream sequence when he asks the custodian of the cemetery not to dig the hole for him in the shade. He seeks at the very least a ray of warm light in a land where the sun plunges into darkness and disfigures. Pasolini, a few years earlier, had spoken of the 'dark sun' in a poem entitled 'Al sole'/'In the Sun' in his collection *La religione del mio tempo*/*The Religion of My Time* (1961).

2 I use the word 'transformations' (*rifacimenti*) between quotation marks. It is the favourite word of Pasolini's mannerism, and also often appears as the title of some of the poems in his 1971 collection *Trasumanar e organizzar*.

The sun is central to Pasolini's myth of nature. There is practically not a single verse, story or text of his in which this light that comes down from the sky is not a consideration. It is fated to exist and it returns in different scenes, from the fields of Friuli to the slums of Rome to the landscapes of Africa. It is not simply the sun dear to Ugo Foscolo[3] that shines on human disasters, but an immemorial, immutable and unattributable light that blankets life and is beyond and contrary to history. '... ah, my only joy is in the sun', Pasolini wrote in a poem emblematically entitled 'La realtà'. In the eternal of the light of the sun, that dies and is reborn, is inscribed the mystery of an existence in its natural state in which the new incessantly repeats the old. 'Billions of the living, / will wake up one sweet morning, / to the simple triumph of the thousands of mornings of life, / with the chain metal shirt ... with the humidity / of the first sweat ...Happy – they are – / happy! Only they so happy! / Only they the possessors of the sun! / The same sun as the barbarian / who descended in the Middle Ages, / and, from mountain gorges, from the shadows / of the snow, made camp / on the thick, black grass / bitter and happy at the coming April.'[4]

The myth of April, recurrent in Pasolini's poems, is linked to the myth of the 'sun of the centuries' that 'shines to death' on bodies forever reborn, in a religious and dreadful silence. April is a further representation of the return, of birth connected to death, that recalls the worship of dawn and spring.[5] The form of Pasolini's poetry pursues and constructs a mythical model of life. The original scene unfolds like an aesthetic one in which style acts as the 'unforgettable awareness of the sun' as a glorified experience of light. The force of the style is able to conflate 'the sun, the real sun, the ferociously ancient sun, / ... with the sun / of film, a pasty grainy grey, / the whiteness of

---

3 Niccolò Ugo Foscolo (1778–1927).

4 'Poesia in forma di rosa' ('Poetry in the Form of a Rose'), in the collection *Poesia in forma di rosa*, Milan: Garzanti, 1964, 57.

5 In one of Pasolini's finest poems, 'Il glicine' ('The Wisteria', 1960, included in his collection *La religione del mio tempo*), the image of April, with its intense sensuality, is embodied in the 'climbing vine' of the title.

destruction, and duplicated, reduplicated / – the sublime sun of memory, / as physical as at the moment / in which it is high in the sky and moves towards / unending sunsets of poverty-stricken countries'.[6] Rays of the sun physically penetrate the lens in Pasolini's film images. 'Making a film is essentially a matter of the sun', Pasolini stated at the end of his *Diario al registratore* during the shooting of *Mamma Roma*.[7] He is not only referring to a technical problem of the light needed for an outdoor shot, but to a sensual immersion in the bodies, in the material forged by light and shadow.

The myth of nature juxtaposed with the sun is called upon to exemplify, more than any other element in the story, a deeply self-conscious side, which Pasolini turns into something lyrical and irrational as if it were an impossibility or a lack of will for him to cross the horizon of the scene of origins. Pasolini is aware of the fact that the deceit of the myth keeps him alive and, above all, keeps his poetry alive.

In *Uccellacci e uccellini*, as already sketched out in *Accattone*, Pasolini treats the subject of the sky as both desired and as a lost possession. He represents it in stylized forms and as parody, forms of awareness and of mediation. The sun fades into a melancholy 'day moon' that significantly acts as the background for the beginning and end titles in the film and at times serves as a backdrop for the moral maxims of the inter-titles. Both the sun and its faded opposite, the moon, have to contend with a mass of clouds in constant motion. Pasolini insists on the strong symbolic charge of this figuration from the very first shot, where the opening titles are accompanied by the singing of Domenico Modugno. After having shown the sky becoming progressively less cloudy and brighter, allowing the moon to shine through, there is a fade which corresponds with the title of the name of the director. The name of Pasolini, who 'by directing, risked his reputation', sets the clouds off on another assault of the moon, turning it as dark as it was at the beginning. Over

6 'L'alba meridionale', in *Poesia in forma di rosa*, 181.
7 See Pier Paolo Pasolini, *Mamma Roma*, Milan: Rizzoli, 1962

the course of the film the two poor protagonists, Totò and Ninetto, turn to the bright star at least twice, but are unable to reach it except in the form of a being on earth encountered in a field and smelling of grass. The name of the 'hooker' is Luna (Moon), an obvious verbal mask, as Stella (Star) is in *Accattone*, the one to whom the pimp Accattone turns and says, ironically and seriously, 'Oh Stella, show me the way!'

Mockingly linking the moon and grass in the episode with the prostitute confounds a degraded scene of origins with a scene of sex. On these two elements, the moonlit sky and the odour of the grassy earth, Pasolini will later construct one of the most touching chapters in *Petrolio*, 'Il pratone della Casilina'.[8] The shadows, the light and the field in *Uccellacci e uccellini* taken together have a strong metaphysical resonance. They provide something more than a set for the mechanical repetition of sex, that mortuary compulsion for reiteration that Pasolini, for the first time, helplessly and disarmingly, represents frontally.

The subject of the religious communion between sky and earth is stylized in *Uccellacci e uccellini* in the form of a comic tale from the past, one of preaching to the birds, told by the crow. In the middle of the ruins of a lost civilization, brother Ciccillo and brother Ninetto stage a parody of what is also a myth from the past. The aesthetic filters are increasingly displayed and their authenticity, as Pasolini would have called it, now passes through the performance of a comic but flat scene.

The progressive desertification of nature is also illustrated with arias in a falsetto voice. There are many shots in which the horizon line divides a barren earth and an empty sky into two perfect halves. Characters are often seen from a great distance as tiny dark background silhouettes, or else are totally absent, which increases the sense of bareness and emptiness.

In the two short films, *La terra vista dalla luna*/*The Earth Seen from the Moon* and *Che cosa sono le nuvole?*/*What Are*

8 *Petrolio* is the unfinished novel by Pasolini, published posthumously in 1992.

Clouds?, heaven and earth, emphasized in the titles, are further subjected to a mannerist mockery. In the first of these films, nature is falsified. Where appearances are not manipulated they seem even more fake. The dead-alive motif and the heaven–earth communion are represented as carnivalesque miracles. The sky in *Che cosa sono le nuvole?* is the 'marvellous, heart-rending beauty of creation', as Totò says at the end of the film. But this striking spectacle of nature is seen from a garbage dump: the sky is the vision and dream of a poet who would still like to confuse life and its representation, reality and illusion, though he knows he cannot.

The desert

In the works of the late 1960s, *Edipo re*, *Teorema*, *Porcile* and *Medea*, Pasolini performed yet another 'transformation' of the scene of origins. From its progressive desertification in the films set in the *borgate*, it shifted to a real and metaphoric image of the desert.

The background of the opening credits of *Teorema* is a desert eaten away by the shadow of clouds in flight. Pasolini, once again, at the opening and close of his films, uses images of the sky or the earth as meaningful signs. He did this in *Uccellacci e uccellini*, and will do so again in *Medea*. In *Teorema*, the image of the desert appears throughout the film at the moments when the characters, disturbed by the visitation of God, flounder about dealing with the violence of the sacred. In the book that accompanies the film (or is accompanied by the film), this open space of wind and sand is theorized as the primordial force of the oneness of the divine and the human. The sky and earth are reversed and each mirrors the other, as the clouds are reflected in Pasolini's shot of the desert.

The desert is the place of original immobility, of a non-progressive journey, of a lack of roads. It represents, not only the point from which one comes and returns, but from which one does not move. On the far and near sides of the desert is nothing but desert. It is by definition an atemporal place, 'a paternal womb' says Pasolini, not a maternal one – in other words, the place of an initial birth that precedes the earthly one in the mother's belly. Finally, it is the place of extreme solitude, both endured and desired. The cry in the desert at the end of the film resounds desperately from nothing towards nothing. The religious experience of this original form of existence is fundamentally portrayed as a nihilist one. It contains a flash of the image of what Pasolini in *Progetto di opere future/Plan for Future Works* (included in his 1964 collection *Poesia in forma di rosa*) defined as 'the obsessive idea of a shiny nothing' and that he referred to seven years later, in a letter to the poet Sandro Penna, as 'the sanctity of nothingness'.

The sights of the desert in *Teorema* need to be interpreted within this ambiguity as an attempt to recreate the myth of the original scene and at the same time as the fundamentally destructive moment that obliterates even as it initiates, an arrival disguised as a point of departure later developed in *La nuova gioventù*, *Salò* and *Petrolio*. These are visions that go well beyond the Friuli mythology, while seeking to merge with it, the reason why the episode of Emilia, entrusted with the task of evoking the sanctity of the ancient birthplace, seems like an old picture lovingly framed but without a future.

Emilia's theorem is the reconstitution of the original unity between sky and earth in equal and opposite movements of ascension and burial. But the image of the buried body is much stronger than that of the levitation. The signs that Pasolini scatters in the shot are more about a nostalgic end of an era than the rehabilitation of a myth. In the shots of the burial there is a mechanical excavator and the hammer and sickle symbols of the Italian Communist Party. Emilia's tears are not to be interpreted as the wailing of the seed that dies only to be resuscitated, according to a peasant and evangelical myth that Pasolini further developed in *Medea*, but needs to be connected to *Il pianto della scavatrice/The Wailing of the Excavator* (1956, included in his collection *Le ceneri di*

Gramsci) in which Pasolini sang of the end of an historical era (post-war and its heritage) and the painful, excruciating weaving together of past, present and future, of dreams that end and dreams destined to begin.

Pasolini concluded the series of films on classical myth with *Medea* (1969). Once again he used a key image placed at the beginning and end of the film, that of the circle. In that shot, the line of the horizon divides the earth from the sky into identical halves, recalling only one other shot in the film when Medea remembers or, better, has a vision of the birth-place she abandoned to follow Jason. The earth is on fire from the sun that ignites it like 'a punch of bloody light'.[9] Once again the image represents the scene of origins shown as a mythical and therefore lost image. Above all, the film repre-sents a visualization of ancient beliefs belonging to peasant culture. In this sense it is one of Pasolini's more theoretical, discursive and mediated works. It directly relates to his theo-ries of the language of reality. Feelings seem permeated by ideas, composed in decorative baroque-like images, except when a landscape is free of figures or when the camera pauses in extreme close-up on the face of Maria Callas.

Outlining the gap between the ancient and the modern, between sacred reality seen as a divine apparition and decon-secrated reality as a heap of meaningless signs, Pasolini is still searching in *Medea* to recover the lost scene of origins through the figure of the double exemplified by the Centaur. The deconsecrated form cannot erase the sacred one preserved beside it or, as in *Petrolio*, beneath it. In *Petrolio*, Pasolini tells the story of the hellish journey of Carlo, the protagonist, who also has his double. He writes of two images embedded in one another. The first is called 'the scene of the vision', a view of the world in 1973. The second is called the 'real scene', the same view of the world but six or seven years earlier when the anthropological catastrophe of consumer culture had not yet occurred or still seemed reversible, and it was still possible

9 These words are from 'La nuova storia', in *Poesia in forma di rosa*, parti-cularly adapted for describing this shot.

to dream about the myth. The scene of the vision of modern horror is deprived of natural colour and light. It covers over the real scene of the past, but not enough to make it invisible. It is like an old neorealist film imprisoned beneath the special effects of a postmodern work.

Destruction

The obsession with the duality of the sacred and the deconsecrated guided the 'remaking' of *La meglio gioventù* into *La nuova gioventù* where Pasolini, overcome in the 1970s by a nihilist rapture, repainted the palette of Friuli in colours opposite to those he had used in the 1940s. In *La nuova gioventù* he established a point of no return until, to his regret and with a self-destructive gesture, he closed both a circle of aesthetic productivity and a vital, personal one. 'Something human is finished', he wrote in his rewriting of *Villotta* from the earlier collection of poetry, *Poesie a Casarsa* (1942).

'I look back and weep over the humble villages, the clouds and the wheat.'[10] Pasolini sings of the end of a 'form of the world' that consisted of the sky, earth and bodies mixed together, of deaths and rebirths, of the eternal return of time. His song is a relentless and sacrilegious destruction of 'a form of poetry', that of the Friuli Garden, irremediably transformed by the arid ugliness of recent history. Not only do the colours, lights and scents of an ancient reality disappear, but so too the prospect of dreaming about them. 'It was not enough to have lost reality, but we had to lose the illusion of it as well!'[11]

The immediate consequence of this irreversible closing of the circle, from *La nuova gioventù* to *La meglio gioventù*, is Pasolini's last film *Salò*, with its gloomy, crystalline horror. It depicts the extreme point of Pasolini's nihilism that was there in waiting since his time in Friuli. Now it no longer

10 'Significato del rimpianto' (part of the 'Tetro entusiasmo' block), *La nuova gioventù*, Turin: Einaudi, 1975, 236.

11 'Poesia popolare' (also part of 'Tetro entusiasmo'), *La nuova gioventù*, 239–240.

had the comfort of reality and its myths. For the first time the scene of origins is not represented. After having previously shot in the open air and often with a hand-held camera and sometimes even directly into the sun, Pasolini now rejects the outdoors. *Salò* is a claustrophobic and glacial work. All roads lead to a void.

In *Petrolio*, more than once, the image of the cosmic flight foreshadows nothingness, the void as the origin and the end. Thus, in the journey on earth in the book, in the notes to the section dedicated to *I godoari*, the hellish desert is encountered where there are still traces of human life but bodies have definitively disappeared.

In the synopsis of *Porno-Teo-Kolossal*, Epifanio, having risen to the sky, cannot find the light of Paradise, but instead a huge black void from which the earth can be seen. He comments: 'Like all the Comets, the Comet I followed was also a stupidity. But without that stupidity, I would never have known you, Earth.' These words lend themselves to be read autobiographically: without my illusions, my poet's myths, I would never have known you earth.

Thus the scene of origins is emptied of bodies, those spring-like bodies of young boys in Friuli, the barbaric ones of the *borgate*, the ancient ones of the Third World and the bodies of all the poor of the world. But this scene cannot entirely disappear for Pasolini, on penalty of Pasolini's own disappearance. He defines himself as 'intoxicated with vegetation and obscurity', a 'poet of the air', who can only speak of odours and colours, of meadows and lights. 'I cry at a dead world. But I who cry for it, am not dead', he wrote in 1973–74 in 'Significato del rimpianto'. A final, spasmodic question springs from out of this scene of ruins: 'Why does the sun remain on the fields?'[12]

The sun, the nether regions, the earth and the poet's solitude are all that resist, painfully, the destruction wrought by history and knowledge.

12 Rewriting of 'Aleluja', in a Poesie a Casarsa, in *La nuova gioventù*, 190.

7 From *Il Decameron* to *Salò*: rewriting

Pasolini's work in the early 1970s can be described by two words: remake and masquerade. They indicate a desire for a play with forms, both joyful and light, opening onto a decade that will continue without him.

Pasolini grouped together *Il decameron/The Decameron* (1971), *I racconti di Canterbury/The Canterbury Tales* (1972) and *Il fiore delle Mille e una notte/Arabian Nights* (1974) with the title *Trilogia della vita/The Trilogy of Life*. It was meant to be playful, like a carnivalesque dance based on motifs and signs of the past. What constitutes the past is not only the world of the common people at the threshold of History made into myth by Pasolini, but also the world of his poetry in the past written in Friulian and in Roman, his stories from the 1950s and his films of the early 1960s. The play is based on the definitive loss of this double past, both existential and aesthetic. Its corollary is an end to any possible projection of a future and consequently the end of any 'obligation', function or role previously assumed by Pasolini.

As far as the labels that Pasolini gave himself, from that of a national-popular writer in the tradition of Gramsci to that of an author for the elite who constructs ambiguous and 'inconsumable' works, the *Trilogia* involves a further displacement with the introduction of the figure of the juggler. The juggler is both transcendent and material, existing between *trasumanar* and *organizzar*.[1] After, provocatively, asserting the uselessness of the poetry of words, that is, of literary poetry, Pasolini sought out the possibility of a journey in film among the ghosts of the past within a 'poetry of reality' he no longer found in the contemporary world. His literary and filmic experience in the early 1970s moves in two distinctly different directions: first, a new experimentalism whose unfinished *monstrum* was to be his novel *Petrolio*; and second, a kind of return to order, albeit provocative, of a realistic objectivity or at least that was the intention. It involved an essentially linear narration that rejected the vertical ups and downs of his earlier films. His poetic and literary efforts during this period seemed to grow out of the fragments of an explosion connected to the demolition of the traditional structures of verse and the novel. It resulted in unusual combinations of elements belonging to different contrasting areas, that of everyday unpoetic speech and the demonstratively literary, the objective and the openly subjective, the complete and incomplete, prosaic legibility and poetic illegibility, the realistic and the allegorical, citation and a 'mad erudite refashioning'.

The film language of the *Trilogia* seems to originate in a desire to recompose matter by choosing familiar modes of representation and narration for the sake of clarity. It was governed by an acceptance of total transparency, the presentation of forms without too much semantic duality, a wilfully direct style, said Pasolini: you see what is visible, narrate what is recountable. In the *Trilogia*, there are no typical or symbolic characters, but simply bodily icons, as there are spatial ones rather than a reconstructed space. The actors do not act, but are limited to reciting prepared dialogue. Their language

---

1 *Trasumanar e organizzar* is the title of Pasolini's 1971 collection of poetry and the title of one of the sections in the collection and one of the poems within it. 'Transumanar' is a citation from Dante (Paradiso I, 70), meaning an internal transformation that allows Dante to describe the celestial realm he is about to enter. A possible translation is 'to go/soar beyond the human'. 'Organizzar' is an excerpt from Left slogans of the period ('organizzare'), almost a cliché. It means 'to organize'.

is like their clothes. It does not easily fit their bodies. The distance between body and words is not filled by voice. Dubbing contributes to radicalize the artifice of representation. Only in *Il Decameron* does language, though still externally placed on bodies, seek a correspondence by the use of dialect or by ornamentation and colouring that is expressive and existential.

The apparent 'linearity' of Pasolini's style consists of a simple alignment and juxtaposition of corporeal, spatial and linguistic elements caught at a moment devoid of temporal development. Though the result seems to be pure realistic fact, immediate, direct and descriptive, it is instead, *ab origine*, already allegorical, fixed, immobilized, a petrified vision of an idea and a feeling. The sense of two-dimensionality, the absence of perspective in *Il Decameron* and the other *Trilogia* films comes from superimposing two levels, both of which are detached from the narrative. On the one hand, there is the material displayed in the *mise en scène* (for example, Franco Citti, who does not so much 'play' Ciappelletto as he is disguised as Ciappelletto). On the other hand, there is the allegorical (Citti is a 'decoration', the perfect example of Pasolini's myth of the common people).[2] The ambiguity of the image has nothing to do with the phenomenology of the real, but belongs to the overlay of allegory and carnivalesque disguise. The Pasolini myth of the common people reaches us somewhat soiled with a caricature-like spasm not contradicting it but rather reconfirming and glorifying it as an object of love.

'I am not writing a factual story, but shaping a form', Pasolini repeated many times in *Petrolio*. The *inventio* of form, particularly in this period, involves the remake and masquerade of other forms. Working with something already formed has been called mannerism and has always been part of Pasolini's poetics. It is central in the *Trilogia* and especially in *Salò*. Remaking is a key word. It contains the seeds of an inescapable obsession and is the basis on which Pasolini's verses are

2 After having played the role in *Accattone*, he appeared in almost all of Pasolini's films.

created and recreated. Condensed in the term is not only an openness to experimentation by Pasolini, who manipulates his own forms and those of others, unlocking them, juxtaposing them well beyond their original place and intention, but also Pasolini's fear of immobility, of not crossing the horizon of his own poetry. Therefore, it is always rewritten, reworked, soiled even, destructured, inverted, but never destroyed.

Behind the aesthetic of the remake lies the philosophy of a return, dear to Pasolini, the desire not to close a horizon, a text or a form. Each return cannot help but be a travesty, as if it were a deformed duplicate. This is the sense that the bodies of the common people in the *Trilogia* assume, those who have become, in Pasolini's words, 'the ghosts of characters from previous realistic films',[3] and, we might add, the ironic and nostalgic semblances of medieval short stories used as the basis for the rewriting. On the other hand and on closer inspection, the previous films, those of the latter half of the 1960s, had not been very different. Greek myth had been used as a disguised form of an idea and a feeling, like an indefinite mirror. The passage from tragedy to comedy, from the classical to the medieval world, imposes a change of style and tone, but does not affect the obsessive nature of the process, that of remaking.

Masquerade in the *Trilogia* is not only central to the creative activity reflecting a process of thought and feeling or, in the Pasolini's words, 'the form of some knowledge', but is also, more concretely and simply, the spirit which guides the *mise en scène*, the ritual underlying the cinema. If the characters of his films on myth were transfigured presences, here they are more noticeably disguised ones. When *Empirismo eretico/Heretical Empiricism* (1972) was first published, with its passionate theses about film as the 'written language of reality', Pasolini wrote a small corollary to it with the *Trilogia*: the cinema is reality, but a 'reality that pokes fun at itself'.[4]

3 Pasolini, 'Il sesso come metafora del potere', *Corriere della Sera*, 25 March 1975.

4 Dario Bellezza, 'Io e Boccaccio, interview with Pasolini', *L'espresso colore*, 22 November 1970, 25.

Like the theatre, it adopts the principle of the staged, disguising, more precisely uncoupling person from character and by so doing creating a slippage between being and representing. No longer is it only a rite of knowledge, but also the place where the rite is performed. The play, according to Pasolini, implies a detachment from reality, an escape experienced as a liberation. As he said to the poet Sandro Penna who was to play Giotto:

> Come and put on this funny costume designed by Danilo Donati just for the fun of it and lend the inexpressible mystery of your physical presence to a mythical Giotto re-evoked just for fun, make him live in your body and you'll see what a time we will have backstage! Or else, tell the soft-drink man in Mergellina: 'Hey, man, come here and put on these gorgeous felt and gold clothes, perform and lend your lively nightingale voice to a certain Riccardo who's been dead for many centuries, and we can play this lovely game together.'[5]

The author inside the work

Paradoxically, in detaching himself from reality, Pasolini entered ever more forcefully into the work. 'I weep for a world already extinct', he wrote in 1974. 'But I who am crying over it am not dead.'[6] Following the collapse of reality, his ego tended to be increasingly tormented, by its invincible solitude, sinking directly, without the slightest mediation, into the texts that became the only certainty for him, one both wretched and sublime. The verses and texts published during this period are dominated by the centrality of the figure of the poet who, like a meteor out of control, disguises himself as a 'custom-made poet', an old 'buffoon', a 'poet of the air'. In *La divina mimesis* (1975), the author plays the role of Dante and, in *Il Decameron*, he 'wears' the eyes of Giotto or, vice versa, lends Giotto his gaze, while in *I racconti di Canterbury* he plays Chaucer.

5 Ibid.
6 Pasolini, 'Significato del rimpianto', *La nuova gioventù*, Turin: Einaudi, 1975, 237.

For some time the objective wholeness that Pasolini professed as a romantic ideal in the 1950s had been shattered. He had hoped to recompose it in the *Trilogia*, albeit in the form of a game. It was certainly no accident that Pasolini, for apparently contingent motives (Penna's refusal to play the role of Giotto), put his own body into *Il Decameron*, a feat entered into under the protection of playful disguise. While 'reality joked with itself', the work became more problematic, albeit under the colours of a carnivalesque structure. If the *Decameron* characters were ghosts released from his previous films, then Pasolini himself in the role of Giotto (or as a northern Italian apprentice to Giotto) was also the marionette-like double of himself who had roamed the slums of Rome in the early 1950s, with a notebook in hand, lighting on reality as if it were a continuous miracle. No longer was reality like an emanation of a religious gaze on the screen, but was instead the comical *mise en scène* of the mechanics of that gaze.

Self-reflective observation is central to *Il Decameron* as it is to the later films of the *Trilogia*. Pasolini wrote in the script:

> What counts are 'Giotto's eyes' a kind of subjectivity that, while looking, takes possession of reality: the reality of the alleys in Naples with their people, objects, gestures, mimicry, situations that we have seen so often in our stories. The faces, the faces, above all, of humble Neapolitans, of a religious people, with their degradation, poverty and sin.

In the scene of Pasolini-Giotto in the middle of the crowded stylized Neapolitan marketplace, bringing his hands to his eyes, in a gesture of framing, in other words, extracting faces from the chaos of daily life to be used in his paintings, he emblematically looked into the camera towards the audience, as if he were outside the film, thereby placing the accent less on the object of his look and more on the act of looking, comically expressed and crudely directed outside the world of the story. The subjective shots of Giotto-Pasolini are false reverse shots. The eye of the great painter, like that of a clown, is a 'divine and observing eye that looks at everything, and transforms everything into something fixed and eternal, that triumphs over time'.[7] This metaphysics of Giotto's gaze is the same that guided Pasolini in his construction of the film's images. The *tableau vivant* of the Last Judgment towards the end of *Il Decameron* represents a sort of key to the interpretation of the entire work. The look becomes transformed into vision and vision becomes an allegorical securing of reality. In fact, the eye does not look, but sees as in a dream. The image is petrified in its expressiveness devoid of any sense of naturalistic time or space. 'Things are seized upon in a moment of such extreme actuality that they seem crystallized or petrified', Pasolini wrote in *Petrolio*; '[e]verything is a series of ornaments or semblances, at the height of their expressivity and at the same time aligned as in Theological Works or Allegories'.[8] This figuration makes itself felt beneath the immediately denotative real. It is emphasized rather than diminished by a constant recourse to the comic, evident particularly in the first two films of the *Trilogia*. Such stylization underlines the image as image, as an icon rather than as a photograph of reality. The game that Pasolini wanted to play with his 'myth of reality' and simultaneously with that of Expression neither relativized nor lessened the status of the image. The shift in tone from the tragic to the grotesque amplified both, sustained by the extremism of the ridiculous and the freedom that resulted from the destructiveness of the comic.

'Amid jokes and games, great truths can emerge', claims the cook with his painted face (clearly a metaphor for the poet-buffoon) at the beginning of *I racconti di Canterbury*. The phrase is less solemn than those Pasolini used in *Porcile* (1969), but functioned similarly as an inscription, a moral summary. Beneath the comic masquerade is an open carnality, the sensuous, the instinctive and, therefore, obscure,

7 These quotations are taken from the continuity secretary's copy of the script, never previously published and preserved in the Fondo Pasolini in Bologna, 263–264.

8 Pasolini, *Petrolio*, Turin: Einaudi, 1992, 182–183.

forsaken and obscene aspects of life. The whole *Trilogia* is based on these 'elementary' substances of existence: the body, both divine and diabolical, with its five senses; dawns and dusks that lend rhythm to a sense of time; youth and old age as part of the circularity of life. And, together with these, a love for the art of the past, not only for the great frescoes and canvases, but the architecture so frequently present in the *Trilogia*: on the one hand, the cathedrals, the medieval small streets and town squares of the West; on the other hand, the enchantment of Oriental cities built in the middle of the desert. This fascination of Pasolini's, evident in his documentary *Le mura di Sana'a/The Walls of Sana'a* (1970–71), shot at the same time as *Il Decameron*, is most evident in the last film of the *Trilogia*, *Il fiore*, sustained by a genuine documentary gift that captures the magic, fabulous nature and concreteness of place. Long shots and extreme long shots of landscapes, already striking in *I racconti*, are increasingly frequent in *Il fiore* by their apparent suspension of emotion in contrast to the grotesque representation of the human figure and of crowds. In *Il fiore* the camera pans along open spaces from a great distance like a dream pervaded by a secret harmony between nature, art and man.

The voyeuristic ritual

Il Decameron and *I racconti di Canterbury* share the same *mise en abyme*: in the former, the haunted eye of Pasolini–Giotto is duplicated by the troubled eye of Citti–Ciappelletto, that is, by Pasolini's former alter ego. The same dialectic between the divine and the demoniacal returns in *I racconti*, where the gaze of Pasolini–Chaucer has its irreverent match with that of Citti, who plays the role of the Devil. In this second film of the *Trilogia*, seeing becomes a true voyeuristic ritual. Citti's most authentic function is that of the gaze of gazes, the peak of a chain of looks. It leads to doubling, tripling, the infinite multiplication of the recurrent voyeuristic scene, more relaxed and dreamlike, even if in *Il fiore* (for example, in the story of Harun and Zeudi) Citti continues to represent the defiance of the devil.

Keeping himself out of the third film of the *Trilogia*, Pasolini allows his gaze to grow calm, abandoning it to the rhythms of an ecstatic vision, no longer having recourse to the comic and the self-reflexiveness it implies. In fact, this is the origin of the greater ability of *Il fiore* (compared to Pasolini's previous films) to reach a sought-after objectivity. By absenting himself from the film, Pasolini allows it to drift like 'a balloon ... in the sky of myth'.[9] Stripping from bodies everything unpleasant as well as their pathos, he suspends them in the unreal colours of an ancient paradise, where the poetic word echoes like elementary music and flesh, harmoniously at one with earth and sky. The subject of the journey which shapes all three films of the *Trilogia* is here, more than ever, initiatory, detached from History and the resistances of consciousness that lead, in *Il Decameron* and *I racconti*, to a constant emphasis on stylization.

In the first film of the *Trilogia* the diverse nature of the physical body of the common people, its non-conformity to the clichés imposed by society, is realized by a grotesque exaggeration of unattractive, unpleasant traits. There are too many grimaces and crooked teeth and too much exaggerated laughter. *Il Decameron*, playing on an obsession with close-ups, has, at certain points, the sense of an ethnographic documentary in which a shattering of the bodily and the gestural almost sadistically place on display the corporeal and the behavioural. The crooked teeth seem scarcely unintentional. They are true and proper deforming, expressionist characteristics.

The carnivalesque *mise en scène* of the public square swarming with bodies and voices directly derived from the texts of Boccaccio and Chaucer is further exaggerated in *I racconti*, where the grotesque is taken to extremes by being linked to the horror and fantastic of traditional Flemish representation. The second film of the *Trilogia* is a doubled, livid reversal of the

9 Bellezza, 'Io e Boccaccio', 14.

18 *The Decameron*. Pasolini in the role of a pupil of Giotto

19 *I racconti di Canterbury*. Pasolini in the role of Chaucer

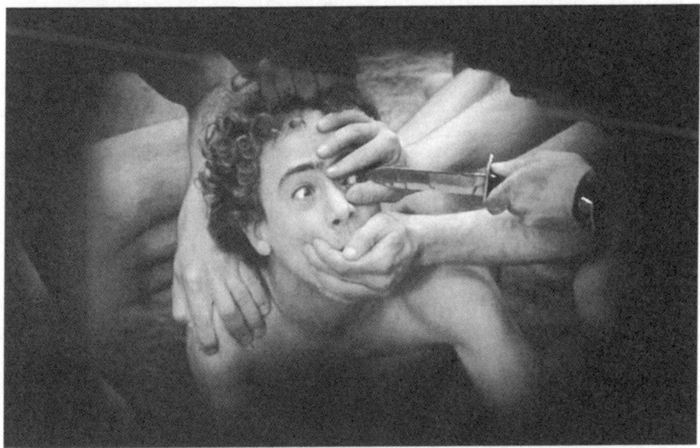

20 *Salò o le 120 giornate de Sodoma*. The final torture sequence

first. It juxtaposes the radiance of the Mediterranean South to the gloom of the North, the saucy freedom and paganism of the body to the scars of martyred, tormented flesh with its taste for transgression and its yearning for sin. If in *Il Decameron* the image of the face prevailed, in *I racconti* its grotesque opposite, the arse, is emphasized with its leitmotiv of farting, having the function in popular culture of desecration associated with the lower body. The two films have almost twin structures in which narration and narrator are interpolated – the narrator is used to link the various episodes, culminating in both with a *tableau vivant*. There is also a rhyming of the two by a similar use of music, song, the confused sound of voices and figurative composition. And there is, above all, the frontal view of beds in distorted perspectives, insistent in both films. In *I racconti*, self-reflectiveness is more troubled and explicit, the references to Pasolini's earlier films more evident by the direct use of citation (the episode with Ninetto Davoli is a perfect example). The two films share common stylistic elements, such as shots taken through a keyhole and shots within shots. There is, too, the series of doors, windows and, especially, arches that frame characters. The voyeuristic *mise en scène* is both obscene (frontal) and aestheticized. It is the first sign of the 'sacred representation' that would inform *Salò* with its extreme *ob scaenam* (infront of the scene) look through binoculars in the final sequence.

Salò, or the 120 Days of Sodom

There is a strong temptation to think of *I racconti* as a prologue to Pasolini's last film, *Salò*. *Il fiore* seems like a parenthesis between two infernos. Actually, the four films from the 1970s form a chain of tightly constructed links. All are reshapings of the other texts and at the same time reflect one another while obeying a single project, that of the work as the summation of other works, a kind of encyclopaedism similar to the idea of *Petrolio*. Not only does one text open to the others but tends to traverse and embrace these. If *Il*

Work on the commentary

By May 1948, Antonio Pietrangeli had already screened 2,000 metres of *La terra trema*, as he mentioned in *La Revue du cinéma*, in a lengthy essay entitled 'Panoramique sur le cinéma italien', in which barely a page was dedicated to Visconti's still unfinished film, but it was a page filled with sharp and enthusiastic observations accompanied by a photograph of the scene of Cola's nocturnal farewell to his sleeping brothers, later edited out of the final version. We cannot automatically conclude from these circumstances that the former assistant director of *Ossessione* had already, by then, been given the task of writing the spoken commentary, since his collaboration with Visconti, beyond their joint commitment to a new Italian cinema, is in itself sufficient to explain this initial contact regarding *La terra trema*. Yet other circumstances make Pietrangeli the ideal candidate for writing that commentary beyond his passionate realist position, his excellent knowledge of Verga's work and the efforts made, on various occasions, to make *I Malavoglia* into a film. In fact, in the early months of 1947, he wrote a twenty-four-page summary of the novel for Universalia Publications which is, actually, a puzzle of critical citations, taken for the most part, but unacknowledged, from the famous study *Giovanni Verga*, by Luigi Russo. In May of the same year, Pietrangeli was busy with the publicity launch of the film version of *I Malavoglia*, as we can see from a document found among his papers, on behalf of the Organizzazione Filmistica Siciliana, a production company in Palermo owned by Francesco and Girolamo Gorgone, which had already produced *Malacarne* (1946) by Pino Mercanti and Giuseppe Zucca, *I cavalieri dalle maschere bianche* (1947) and *Il principe ribelle* (1947), both by Mercanti. On 21 June 1947, an article by Pietrangeli with an emblematic title was published in *Fotogrammi*: 'I Malavoglia di Verga sullo schermo. Personaggi che aspettano'. The article burns with the same feeling and on the same ideal lines that had previously, six years earlier, been present in the famous articles by Mario Alicata and Giuseppe De Santis in *Cinema*: 'Verità e poesia: Verga e il cinema italiano' and 'Ancora di Verga e del cinema italiano'.

'And where would we find', wrote Pietrangeli, 'the thread of a narrative tradition to which the Italian cinema could be part of? Perhaps in the spiritualist-sensual-Darwinian-mystical adventures of the tepid and fearful [*tiepido e trepido*] heroes of Fogazzaro? Or in the desperate and bitter events of the Malavoglia, in the suffering, tears and sweat of those "poor people" who love without hope, die without justice, endure without kindness, grasping the few stones that are the "house by the medlar tree", and like, for months and years, the sounds of the monotonous pounding of the waves against the Faraglioni ... Today, 'Ntoni as Master 'Ntoni, Mastro Don Gesualdo, La Lupa, Feli – a parade of human characters, sparkling with shimmering glances, aflame with passions, frozen with desperation – waiting to be put on screen.' *La terra trema* fulfils that task, though in the credits there is no mention of Verga, while the spoken commentary, in particular, finds in Verga's masterpiece something more than a literary reference. It uses it as a source of formulas, phrases and, more profoundly, meanings and visions of the world.

The complex development of the script, which went through four drafts, exhibited Visconti's usual concern for details in work done at the margins of the film, externally to it and almost contrary to it. At the same it testifies to the careful attention to language, which certainly took as its model the methods of Verga. The passage from the first version to the last can be understood as a progressive drawing near to Verga. It takes place on two levels, one lexical-phraseological and the other morphological-syntactical. The first concerns manners of phrasing, the use of adjectives, adverbs and the considerable use of proverbs.

We shall limit ourselves to a few examples:

COMMENTARY

Buontempo e maltempo non dura tutto il tempo. E ormai il mare non sembra nemmeno più quello che s'è portato via la barca di 'Ntoni. (Good weather and bad weather do not last forever. Now

Decameron and *I racconti* represent the South–North diptych of the civilized West, then *Il fiore* is the Eastern, Third World other side. All are chapters, variations, details on the same themes: that of the body of the common people, the act of narration, and the nature of reality and of narration as these pass through different cultures and philosophies. They move from forms of the mythic and the religious that dominated the films that immediately preceded the *Trilogia* to oral narration characteristic of the three. The formula chosen by Pasolini is that of a story within a story, with the narration left to an outside narrator or, best of all, to a true multiplicity of voices. If his fascination with the oral form is clear, involving the relation of the voice to the body and of knowledge to life, just as clear is the choice of a narrator coming from the common people and therefore different from himself. It recalls Pasolini's disguise of speaking through the voice of others or directly entering as a *deus ex machina*, as occurs in the first two films of the *Trilogia*. Masquerade is a mechanism of doubling, as is mediation. In *Il Decameron*, for example, Pasolini spoke through Boccaccio, and Boccaccio through his character narrators. The 'endless narrating', of 'one thing after another and one inside the other, to infinity',[10] is the model for his unfinished *Petrolio* that derives, as Pasolini stated, directly from *Il fiore*, a reference once more to the idea of the *summa*, a perpetually open work as an intersection of other works and the synthesis of Pasolini's own knowledge.

Salò can be included in this project. It 'emotionally' overturns the world of meanings in the *Trilogia*, while constituting a continuation of it along the lines of an exploration between the body and a narrative of the body. It takes to Sadian extremes the idea of the oral as a definitive purification of History, and therefore of stories, in an obscene religious equation of the Word made flesh. By means of allegory, mediated by recourse to the Boccaccio–Chaucer diptych, the figurative repertory of medieval art and the destructive power of laughter, Pasolini addressed the idea of the exuberant as an

---

10 Quoted in *Lettere 1955–1975*, Turin: Einaudi, 1988, 152.

infraction of social and cultural codes. It crosses the threshold of consent, to make excess explode as transgression. This becomes increasingly radical from one film to the next, until it reaches its peak in *Salò*. In *Il Decameron*, Masetto's tumescent sex, seen in a subjective shot from below by the nuns, is a sacred apparition, a sort of tabernacle, a substitute icon for Christ. The view is reversed in the final sequence of torture in *Salò*. It is the blasphemous Christ of Sade, like a haloed voyeur, with his binoculars, looking down from above, at a Bosch-like inferno of butchered flesh. The device of 'sacred representation' invoked by Pasolini is left intact. The body remains at the centre, the divine and demoniacal drive of flesh moves from the intentionally transgressive and joyful forms of the earlier films to become martyrdom, torture and crucifixion.

With respect to the *Trilogia*, *Salò* has the same role of *La nuova gioventù* in relation to *La meglio gioventù*. It is a reshaping as a negative, a reflection of the same in reverse. Once upon a time the body was linked to the rituals of archaic communities, anchored to a religious concept of existence. In *Salò*, the rituals are transformed into ceremonials, the pulse of life and its sacral substance into a cold geometry of shapes. Within a theatrical space, enclosed by obsessive symmetries, actions and gestures are repeated, accumulate and duplicated incessantly. As Pasolini stated, *Salò* has the refractory and severe nature of a crystal. After the brief realistic prologue involving the fascist round-up, Pasolini offers the viewer variations of the same claustrophobic ceremony. Mixing together Sade and Dante, the allegorical dimension of the film is articulated in an anti-inferno and infernal circles dedicated respectively to manias, shit and blood. Characters are reduced to functions: four men who represent economic, religious, aristocratic and judiciary power and four women charged with officiating at the ceremonies as narrators and musical accompanists. Together they evoke bordello *maîtresses* and cabaret actresses. Disposed around these figures are eight female and eight male victims,

accompanied by a chorus of soldiers, servants and collaborators. The dialogue reproduces the words of Sade's text, and
phrases from Pierre Klossowski and Roland Barthes, whose
essays on Sade are cited in the *Essential Bibliography* inserted
in the titles of the film, along with texts by Maurice Blanchot,
Simone de Beauvoir and Philippe Sollers.

Salò can be interpreted as a grotesque and violent 'Reality
TV' show as the Italian poet Gianni D'Elia suggested. The
entry into the villa with its priests (the four libertines) and
entertainers (the four madams), the simulations, progressive nominations and eliminations of the 'victims' lead
towards a totalitarian horizon where true and the false are
confounded in repetitive and obscene performances. Everything is abstractly premeditated, perfectly calculated, subject
to a continuous game of material and symbolic masquerade.
The Fascist power of the Salò Republic becomes a metaphor
for the power of television, the incarnation of the 'unreality' of the contemporary world and it assumes an ahistoric
dimension. The atemporality of the film is reflected in
the repetitiveness of its narrative form and in the obsessive re-presentation of the same spatial and bodily figures.
Victims and torturers tend to become confused in a circular movement that reproduces the situation between audience and programmer in television, as if we now live in an
eternal and horrendous TV show. In the final sequence of
the torturing, the look of the viewer becomes identified with
that of the torturer. The camera seems to simulate live television with a zoom lens pointed, with cold and pathological
satisfaction, towards one of the contemporary world's many
massacres. Pasolini exhibits what can only be viewed, if not
by a totally indifferent look, by an exaggerated thrill. It is the
contrary of the torture scene in Rossellini's *Roma città aperta*
(1945) that confronts the viewer as if it were an initiation.
Serge Daney referred to it as a modern gaze, a product of the
revelation and consciousness of the horror of history. *Salò*, to
the contrary, can be thought of as establishing a postmodern
gaze – were it not for the inadequacy of the term – that is,

one constituted by the anarchy, lack of conscience, indifference and omnipotence of the horror of television. In *Salò*, the body is transformed into flesh on display, definitively losing its mythical aura in exchange for the immaterial and violent nature of media icons. If, in the *Trilogia*, flesh still signified a disdain towards power, in *Salò* it is power that reduces flesh to 'religious' consumption.

Juxtaposed to an excess of life, as the reverse side of the same coin, it is an excess of death. Everything that was intentionally a joyful overflowing of meaning is transformed into a harrowing emptying of meaning. The body, retouched and repeated, becomes progressively more obscure and indecipherable. As Pasolini wrote in *La divina mimesis*:

> The repetition of a feeling becomes an obsession. And the obsession transforms feeling … Like the repetition of a word in litanies … Repetition as the loss of meaning and the loss of meaning as meaning … Exhilarating … Ha, ha ha.[11]

Reiteration in *Salò* is central, even from figurative and structural points of view. The film, which began as a philosophical treatise about the destruction of the body (and of reality and History) pursued it by means of insatiable hyperbole. And it was precisely that gesture of annihilation by excess that provoked and recreated a gigantic corporeal superabundance. At the moment in which the body is no more, there is nothing else but body.

The nihilistic urge for power that Pasolini stages in the film is like his own projection beyond any acceptable schema, project, code or ideology. The nullification by excess is the monstrous value that resists the collapse of all values. For this reason the film is not only a challenge to what can be represented but, sinking ever deeper into an abyss, a challenge to being itself. For Pasolini, pushing the visible to its limits also involves crossing the boundary between being and nothingness, thereby touching on the mystery that existence shares with art against the false paradigms of History. One of

11 Pasolini, *La divina mimesis*, Turin: Einaudi, 1975, 18.

the titles entertained for *Salò* was 'Dada', as an ironic pastiche between the name of the historical avant-garde movement and the jingle 'Du-Du-Dufour' in the advertising campaign for a brand of chocolates. The verbal game versus logical meanings ('Salò = salaud *fr.* [bastard]', Pasolini remarked, jokingly) becomes an attack on meaning, on accepted and proven codes, keeping the mystery of meaning open as a circular movement of opposites, of affirmation and negation, fullness and emptiness, life and death. More than this being a matter of the unrepresentable, it is more the case of illegibility, a term Pasolini used over and over again in his literary works to evoke that mystery. The Sadian and Dantesque descents into hell are presented as a descent into the aberrations of History and also as an abandonment of the self to the mysterious drives of the unconscious.

Had the tragic death of Pasolini not thrown a ghastly veil over *Salò*, it might have been easier to see the degree of excitement and liberation inscribed in its nihilist gesture. It is not only an act of impotence and refusal but of omnipotence as the will to avoid surrender and the definitive collapse of illusions and its rules. All the energy Pasolini devoted during those years to repudiation (of the peasant world of Friuli in *La meglio gioventù*, of the popular universe of the *Trilogia*, of the general 'unreality' of the present) is symptomatic of a twofold movement. The more he removed himself from History, the more he continued to 'throw his own body into the struggle', into the midst of things. His *Scritti corsari* are direct evidence of this attitude one might define with the overused terms of 'civil' and 'uncivil', of involvement and accession in current events. A *trasumanar e organizzar*, as Pasolini said, evoking Dante. Looked at more closely, these journalistic writings are a translation into political terms and into a philosophy of History of the terrible and intoxicating illegibility of *Salò* and therefore they remain on the near side of the threshold that the film breaches. It was preferable that Pasolini's testamentary bequest be entrusted to the legibility of this writing, as ambiguous as it may be, thereby charging it with an aura of prophecy. While History seems to have surpassed even the nihilism of the early 1970s, in terms of degradation and dehumanization, *Salò*, with its obscene mystery, its sacral violence, its *trasumanar* in the meshes of raw flesh, continues to be the *monstrum* that everyone has seen without being able to look at. Too often the unbearable image, which in its extreme state even exceeded pornography, has erected a shield against the idea underlying it. This detailed visual substance can be confused with the mass of flesh that the cinema, because of its referential nature, brings to the foreground. In fact, no one ever dreamed of reproaching Dante or Bosch, as has happened to Pasolini, for the horrendous force of their representations. No different than its precedents, *Salò* is the vision of the world of a poet who, in an aroused and excessive fantasy, cloaks a speculative torment in sexual garb. *Salò*, close to both Sade and Dante, is not only an allegory of the contemporary world, but expresses, more radically and obscurely, a philosophical position on the nature of being.

More than thirty years after *Salò*, we can still regret having not been able to see the 'reshaping', which surely would have existed, of this final crossing, in the biblical sense, of the desert.

Select filmography

Paisà/*Paisan* (1946), 126 min.

Director: Roberto Rossellini

Assistant directors: Federico Fellini, Massimo Mida, Eugenia Handamir, Annalena Limentani

Producers: Roberto Rossellini (OFI), Rod E. Geiger (FFP)

Production companies: Organizzazione Film Internazionali (OFI), Foreign Film Productions (FFP)

Production manager: Ugo Lombardi

Story: Sergio Amidei with the collaboration of Klaus Mann, Federico Fellini, Marcello Pagliero, Alfred Hayes, Roberto Rossellini

Script: Sergio Amidei, Federico Fellini, Roberto Rossellini (adaptation and English translation: Annalena Limentani)

Photography (black and white): Otello Martelli

Direct sound: Ovidio Del Grande

Editor: Eraldo Da Roma

Music: Renzo Rossellini

Cast includes: Sicily episode: Carmela Sazio (Carmela), Robert Van Loon (Joe); Naples episode: Alfonsino Bovino (Pasquale), Dotts M. Johnson (Joe); Rome episode: Maria Michi (Francesca), Gar Moore (Fred); Florence episode: Harriet White (Harriet), Renzo Avanzo (Massimo); Romagna episode: Bill Tubbs (Father Bill Martin); Po Delta episode: Dale Edmonds (Dale).

First screening: 18 September 1946, Venice Film Festival.

Released: 10 December 1946, Turin; 4 February 1948, New York; 12 October 1948, London.

La terra trema (1948), 161 min.

Director: Luchino Visconti

Assistant directors: Francesco Rosi, Franco Zeffirelli

Producer: Salvo D'Angelo

Production company: Universalia Produzione

Production managers: Anna Davini, Renato Silvestri

Story: Luchino Visconti [loosely adapted from the novel *I malavoglia*, 1881 (*The House by the Medlar Tree*), by Giovanni Verga]

Script, dialogues and commentary: Luchino Visconti, Antonio Pietrangeli

Photography (black and white): G. R. Aldo

Direct sound: Vittorio Trentino

Music: coordinated by Luchino Visconti and Willy Ferrero and performed under the direction of Willy Ferrero

Editor: Mario Serandrei

Cast (uncredited) *includes*: Antonio Arcidiacono ('Ntoni), Giuseppe Arcidiacono (Cola), Nelluccia Giammona (Mara), Agnese Giammona (Lucia), Rosario Galvagno (Don Salvatore), Nicola Castorino (Nicola), Rosa Costanzo (Nedda), and other inhabitants of the village of Aci Trezza.

First screening: 2 September 1948, Venice Film Festival.

Il Gattopardo/*The Leopard* (1963), 187 min.

Director: Luchino Visconti

Assistant directors: Rinaldo Ricci, Albino Cocco

Producer: Goffredo Lombarto (Titanus)

Production companies: Titanus (Roma), SGC, SN Pathé Cinéma (Paris)

Production managers: Enzo Provenzale, Giorgio Adriani

Story: from the novel of the same title by Giuseppe Tomasi di Lampedusa

Script: Luchino Visconti, Suso Cecchi d'Amico, Enrico Medioli, Pasquale Festa Campanile, Massimo Franciosa
Photography (Technirama, Technicolor): Giuseppe Rotunno
Art direction: Mario Garbuglia
Set decoration: Giorgio Pes, Laudomia Hercolani
Costumes: Piero Tosi
Music: Nino Rota, and an unpublished waltz by Giuseppe Verdi
Editor: Mario Serandrei
Cast includes: Burt Lancaster (Prince Don di Fabrizio di Salina), Alain Delon (Tancredi), Claudia Cardinale (Angelica Sedara), Rina Morelli (Maria Stella, wife of Prince Salina), Paolo Stoppa (Don Calogero Sedara), Romolo Valli (Father Pirrone), Lucilla Morlacchi (Concetta), Ida Galli (Carolina), Pierre Clementi, Carlo Valenzano, Anna Maria Bottini, Mario Girotti, Serge Reggiani, Brock Fuller, Ivo Garrani, Giuliano Gemma, Leslie French, Ottavia Piccolo, Rina De Liguoro.
First screening: 28 March 1963, Rome.

Vaghe stelle dell'Orsa ... (1965), 100 min.
Of a Thousand Delights, UK
Sandra, USA

Director: Luchino Visconti
Assistant director: Albino Cocco
Producer: Franco Cristaldi (Vides)
Production company: Vides
Executive producer: Oscar Brazzi
Production manager: Sergio Merolle
Story and script: Luchino Visconti, Suso Cecchi d'Amico, Enrico Medioli
Photography (black and white): Armando Nannuzzi
Art direction: Mario Garbuglia
Set decoration: Laudomia Hercolani
Costumes: Bice Brichetto
Music: 'Prelude, Chorale and Fugue' (César Franck)

Songs: 'Io che non vivo senza te' (Donaggio-Pallavicini), 'Una rotonda sul mare' (Migliacci-Faleni), 'E se domani ...' (Giorgio Calabrese-Carlo Alberto Rossi), 'Strip-Cinema' (Pino Calvi), 'Let's Go' and 'If You Don't Want' performed by Le Tigri

Editor: Mario Serandrei

Cast includes: Claudia Cardinale (Sandra), Jean Sorel (Gianni), Michel Craig (Andrew), Renzo Ricci (Gilardini), Marie Bell (mother of Sandra and Gianni), Fred Williams (Pietro), Amalia Troiani (Fosca).

First screening: 3 September 1965, Venice Film Festival.

Il Decameron/*The Decameron* (1971), 110 min.

Director: Pier Paolo Pasolini

Assistant directors: Sergio Citti, Umberto Angelucci

Producer: Franco Rossellini

Production companies: PEA (Roma), Les Productions Artistes Associés (Paris), Artemis Film (Berlin)

Executive producer: Alberto De Stefanis

Production manager: Mario Di Biase

Story and script: Pier Paolo Pasolini, based on Giovanni Boccaccio's 'Il Decameron'

Photography (Eastmancolor): Tonino Delli Colli

Art direction: Dante Ferretti

Set decoration: Andrea Fantacci

Costumes: Danilo Donati

Music: coordinated by Pasolini, with the collaboration of Ennio Morricone: 'Canto delle lavandaie del Vomero' by anonymous of the thirteenth century, old and new popular Neapolitan songs

Editors: Nino Baragli, Tatiana Casini Morigi

Cast includes: Franco Citti (Ciappelletto), Ninetto Davoli (Andreuccio da Perugia), Jovan Jovanovic (Rustico), Vincenzo Amato (Masetto), Angela Luce (Peronella), Pier Paolo Pasolini (Giotto's pupil), Guido Alberti (a rich merchant), Gianni Rizzo (Friar Superior), Giuseppe

Zigaina (Friar confessor), Elisabetta Genovese (Caterina), Silvana Mangano (the Madonna).

First screening: 29 June 1971, Berlin Film Festival.

I racconti di Canterbury/*The Canterbury Tales* (1972),
   110 min.

Director: Pier Paolo Pasolini

Assistant directors: Sergio Citti, Umberto Angelucci

Producer: Alberto Grimaldi

Production company: PEA (Roma)

Production manager: Alessandro von Normann

Story and script: Pier Paolo Pasolini, based on Geoffrey Chaucer's 'The Canterbury Tales'

Photography (Eastmancolor-Technicolor): Tonino Delli Colli

Art direction: Dante Ferretti

Set decoration: Kenneth Muggleston

Costumes: Danilo Donati

Music: coordinated by Pasolini, with the collaboration of Ennio Morricone: 'Fenesta ca lucive' by anonymous, popular Irish and English songs, other themes elaborated by Ennio Morricone

Editors: Nino Baragli, Tatiana Casini Morigi

Cast includes: Hugh Griffith (Sir January), Laura Betti (the Wife of Bath), Franco Citti (the Devil), Ninetto Davoli (Perkin), Josephine Chaplin (May), John Francis Lane (Monk), Alan Webb (the old man), J. P. Van Dyne (Cook), Pier Paolo Pasolini (Chaucer).

First screening: 2 July 1972, Berlin Film Festival.

Il fiore delle Mille e una notte/*Arabian Nights* (1974),
   129 min

Director: Pier Paolo Pasolini

Assistant directors: Umberto Angelucci, Peter Shepherd

Producer: Alberto Grimaldi

Production companies: PEA (Roma)/Les Productions Artistes Associés (Paris)

Production manager: Mario Di Biase

Story and script: Pier Paolo Pasolini, based on *The Arabian Nights*

Photography (Eastmancolor): Giuseppe Ruzzolini

Art direction: Dante Ferretti

Costumes: Danilo Donati

Music: Ennio Morricone

Editors: Nino Baragli, Tatiana Casini Morigi

Cast includes: Ninetto Davoli (Aziz), Franco Citti (the Demon), Franco Merli (Nur-ed-Din), Tessa Bouché (Aziza), Ines Pellegrini (Zumurrud).

First screening: 20 May 1974, Cannes Film Festival.

Salò o le 120 giornate di Sodoma (1975), 116 min.

Director: Pier Paolo Pasolini

Assistant director: Umberto Angelucci

Producer: Alberto Grimaldi

Production companies: PEA (Roma)/Les Productions Artistes Associés (Paris)

Executive producer: Alberto De Stefanis

Production manager: Antonio Girasante

Story and script: Pier Paolo Pasolini, with the collaboration of Sergio Citti and Pupi Avati, based on the Marquis de Sade's novel *Les 120 Journées de Sodome*

Photography (Eastmancolor-Technicolor): Tonino Delli Colli

Art direction: Dante Ferretti

Set decoration: Osvaldo Desideri

Costumes: Danilo Donati

Music coordinated by: Ennio Morricone

Music: Fryderyk Chopin 'Preludio in mi min', op. 28 n. 4 'Valzer in la min.', op. 34 n. 2), Carl Orff ('Carmina Burana') and the songs: 'Son tanto triste', 'Tu amore', 'Tu sei la musica' by Francesco Ansaldo and Alfredo Bracchi; 'Fiori d'arancio', 'Maestro improvvisa' by Giovanni D'Anzi and Michele Galdieri; 'Dormi bambina' by Corrado Pintaldi and Enzo Bonfanti; 'Valzer di mezzanotte' by

Frank Amodio and Michele Cittadino; 'Quel motivetto che mi piace tanto' by Donato Casolaro and Michele Galdieri; 'Settembre ti dirà' by Antonio Moretti; 'Torna piccina mia' by Cesare Bixio and Andrea Bixio; 'Canzone del platano' by Giuseppe Barzizza and Riccardo Morbelli; 'Stelius Alpinis' by Enrico Zardini

Editors: Nino Baragli, Tatiana Casini Morigi

Cast includes: *Signori*: Paolo Bonacelli (the Duke Blangis), Giorgio Cataldi (the Bishop, dubbed by Giorgio Caproni), Uberto Paolo Quintavalle (Magistrate Curval), Aldo Valletti (President Durcet, dubbed by Marco Bellocchio). *Narrators*: Caterina Boratto (Mrs Castelli), Elsa de' Giorgi (Mrs Maggi), Hélène Surgère (Mrs Vaccari, dubbed by Laura Betti), Sonia Saviange (pianist).

First screening: 22 November 1975, Paris.

Select bibliography

This bibliography is a selection of major studies on themes, authors and films discussed in this volume. Only books and magazine special issues are included, with no mention of essays in books or in magazines. As for directors, only books on their entire career or on the films analysed in this volume are included.

Cesare Zavattini

Bernardini, Aldo and Jean Gili (eds), *Cesare Zavattini* (Paris: Centre Georges Pompidou, 1990).

Gambetti, Giacomo, *Zavattini mago e tecnico* (Rome: Ente dello Spettacolo, 1986).

Masoni, Tullio and Paolo Vecchi (eds), *Zavattini Cinema* (Bologna: Analisi, 1988).

Moneti, Guglielmo (ed.), *Lessico zavattiniano. Parole e idee su cinema e dintorni* (Venice: Marsilio, 1992).

Nuzzi, Paolo (ed.), *Una vita Za. Le opere e i giorni di Cesare Zavattini. Giornalismo, letteratura, cinema* (Parma: Guanda, 1995).

Nuzzi, Paolo and Ottavio Iemma, *De Sica e Zavattini. Parliamo tanto di noi* (Rome: Editori Riuniti, 1997).

Parigi, Stefania, *Fisiologia dell'immagine. Il pensiero di Cesare Zavattini* (Turin: Lindau, 2006).

Zavattini, Cesare, *Basta coi soggetti!*, ed. Roberta Mazzoni (Milan: Bompiani, 1979).

Zavattini nella città del cinema, special issue of *Cinema e Cinema*, 20 (July–September 1979).

Zavattini, Cesare, *Neorealismo ecc.*, ed. Mino Argentieri (Milan: Bompiani, 1979). Also published in Cesare Zavattini, *Opere cinema* (Milan: Bompiani, 2002).

Zavattini, Cesare, *Diario cinematografico*, ed. Valentina Fortichiari (Milan: Bompiani, 1979 and Milan: Mursia, 1991). Also published in Cesare Zavattini, *Opere cinema* (Milan: Bompiani, 2002).

Zavattini, Cesare, *Opere 1931–1986*, ed. Silvana Cirillo (Milan: Bompiani, 1991).

Zavattini, Cesare, *Uomo, vieni fuori!*, ed. Orio Caldiron (Rome: Bulzoni, 2006).

Roberto Rossellini

Aprà, Adriano (ed.), *Rosselliniana. Bibliografia internazionale. Dossier 'Paisà'* (Entre Mostra Internazionale del Nuovo Cinema, Rome: Di Giacomo Editore, 1987).

Aprà, Adriano (ed.), *Il dopoguerra di Rossellini* (Rome: Cinecittà International, 1995).

Aprà, Adriano, *In viaggio con Rossellini* (Alessandria: Falsopiano, 2006).

Baldelli, Pio, *Roberto Rossellini* (Rome: La Nuova Sinistra-Samonà e Savelli, 1972).

Bergala, Alain and Jean Narboni (eds), *Roberto Rossellini* (Paris: Editions de l'Etoile–Cahiers du Cinéma, 1990).

Bondanella, Peter, *The Films of Roberto Rossellini* (New York: Cambridge University Press, 1993).

Brunette, Peter, *Roberto Rossellini* (New York, Oxford: Oxford University Press, 1987).

Bruno, Edoardo (ed.), *Roberto Rossellini. Il cinema, la televisione, la storia, la critica* (Sanremo: Città di Sanremo, 1980).

Degener, David, *Sighting Rossellini* (Berkeley: University Art Museum–University of California Press, 1973).

Forgacs, David, Sarah Lutton and Geoffrey Nowell-Smith (eds), *Roberto Rossellini. Magician of the Real* (London: BFI, 2000).

Gallagher, Tag, *The Adventures of Roberto Rossellini. His Life and Films* (New York: Da Capo Press, 1998).

Guarner, José Luis, *Roberto Rossellini* (London: Studio Vista, 1970).

Hovald, Patrice G., *Roberto Rossellini* (Bruxelles: Club du Livre de Cinéma, 1958).

Iaccio, Pasquale (ed.), *L'utopia concreta di Roberto Rossellini* (Naples: Liguori, 2006).

Masi, Stefano and Enrico Lancia, *I film di Roberto Rossellini* (Rome: Gremese, 1987).

Meder, Thomas, *Vom Sichtbarmachen der Geschichte: der italienisch 'neorealismus', Rossellini's 'Paisà' und Klaus Mann* (Munich: Trickster, 1993).

Menon, Gianni (ed.), *Dibattito su Rossellini* (Rome: Partisan, 1972).

Parigi, Stefania (ed.), Paisà. *Analisi del film* (Venice: Marsilio, 2005).

Quintana, Àngel, Jos Oliver and Settimio Presutto (eds), *Roberto Rossellini. La herencia de un maestro* (Valencia: Institut Valencià de Cinematografia–Filmoteca de Catalunya–Filmoteca Española, 2005).

Ranvaud, Don (ed.), *Roberto Rossellini* (London: BFI, 1981).

Rondolino, Gianni, *Roberto Rossellini* (Turin: UTET, 1989).

Rossellini, Roberto, *The Trilogy of War*, ed. Stefano Roncoroni, trans. Judith Green (New York: Grossman and London: Lorrimer, 1973).

Rossellini, Roberto, *Le Cinéma révélé*, ed. Alain Bergala (Paris: Editions de l'Etoile–Cahiers du Cinéma, 1984).

Rossellini, Roberto, *My Method. Writings and Interviews*, ed. Adriano Aprà (New York: Marsilio, 1992).

Serceau, Michel, *Roberto Rossellini* (Paris: Editions du Cerf, 1986).

Wagstaff, Christopher *Italian Neorealist Cinema. An Aesthetic Approach* (Toronto: University of Texas Press, 2007).

Luchino Visconti

Bacon, Henry, *Visconti. Explorations of Beauty and Decay* (Cambridge: Cambridge University Press, 1998).

Baldelli, Pio, *Luchino Visconti* (Milan: Mazzotta, 1973).

Bianchi, Pietro (ed.), *Vaghe stelle dell'Orsa ...* (Bologna: Cappelli, 1965).

Bruni, David and Veronica Pravadelli (eds), *Studi viscontiani* (Venice: Marsilio, 1997).

Cecchi d'Amico, Suso (ed.), *Il film 'Il Gattopardo' e la regia di Luchino Visconti* (Bologna: Cappelli, 1963).

De Giusti, Luciano, *I film di Luchino Visconti* (Rome: Gremese, 1985).

Estève, Michel (ed.), *Luchino Visconti. L'histoire et l'esthétique*, special issue of *Etudes cinématographiques* 26–27 (Autumn 1963).

Ishaghpour, Youssef, *Visconti. Le sens et l'image* (Paris: Editions de la Différence, 1984).

Lagny, Michèle (ed.), *Classicisme et subversion* (Paris: Publications de la Sorbonne Nouvelle, 1990).

Liandrat-Guigues, Suzanne, *Les Images du temps dans 'Vaghe stelle dell'Orsa...' de Luchino Visconti* (Paris: Presses de la Sorbonne Nouvelle, 1995).

Micciché, Lino, *Visconti e il neorealismo. Ossessione, La terra trema, Bellissima* (Venice: Marsilio, 1990).

Micciché, Lino (ed.), *La terra trema di Luchino Visconti. Analisi di un capolavoro* (Turin: Associazione Philip Morris Progetto Cinema–Centro Sperimentale di Cinematografia–Lindau, 1993).

Micciché, Lino (ed.), *Il Gattopardo* (Naples: Electa–Centro Sperimentale di Cinematografia, 1996).

Micciché, Lino, *Luchino Visconti. Un profilo critico* (Venice: Marsilio, 1996).

Montesanti, Fausto (ed.), *Luchino Visconti. La terra trema* (shot-by-shot analysis), *Bianco e Nero* 2–3 (February–March 1951).

Nowell-Smith, Geoffrey, *Luchino Visconti* (London: BFI, 2003).

Pravadelli, Veronica (ed.), *Il cinema di Luchino Visconti* (Roma: Biblioteca di Bianco, and Nero–Quaderni 2, 2000).

Pravadelli, Veronica (ed.), *Visconti a Volterra. La genesi di Vaghe stelle dell'Orsa* ... (Turin: Philip Morris–Lindau, 2000).

Renzi, Renzo, *Visconti segreto* (Bari: Laterza, 1994).

Rondolino, Gianni, *Visconti* (Turin: UTET, 1982).

Schifano, Laurence, *Luchino Visconti. Les feux de la passion* (Paris: Libraire Académique Perrin, 1987).

Schifano, Laurence, *Le Guépard* (Poitiers: Nathan, 1991).

Tonetti, Claretta, *Luchino Visconti* (Boston: Twayne, 1983).

Ungari, Enzo (ed.), *La terra trema* (Bologna: Cappelli, 1977).

Pier Paolo Pasolini

Betti, Laura and Michele Gulinucci (eds), *Le regole di un'illusione* (Rome: Fondo Pier Paolo Pasolini, 1991).

Bergala, Alain and Jean Narboni (eds), *Pasolini cinéaste*, special issue of *Cahiers du Cinéma* (1981).

De Giusti, Luciano, *I film di Pier Paolo Pasolini* (Roma: Gremese, 1983).

Di Giammatteo, Fernaldo (ed.), *Lo scandalo Pasolini*, special issue of *Bianco e Nero* (January–April 1976).

Duflot, Jean (ed.), *Entretiens avec Pier Paolo Pasolini* (Paris: Belfond, 1970). Later expanded as *Les dernières paroles d'un impie* (Paris: Belfond, 1981).

Estève, Michel (ed.), *Pasolini 1 – Le Mythe et le sacré*, special issue of *Etudes cinématographiques* 109–111 (1976).

Estève, Michel (ed.), *Pasolini 2 – Un 'cinéma de poésie'*, special issue of *Etudes cinématographiques* 112–114 (1977).

Ferrero, Adelio, *Il cinema di Pier Paolo Pasolini* (Venice: Marsilio, 1977).

Fortini, Franco, *Attraverso Pasolini* (Turin: Einaudi, 1993).

Gérard, Fabien S., *Pasolini ou le mythe de la barbarie* (Bruxelles: Edition de l'Université de Bruxelles, 1981).

Gervais, Marc, *Pier Paolo Pasolini* (Paris: Seghers, 1973).

Greene, Naomi, *Pier Paolo Pasolini: Cinema as Heresy* (Princeton: Princeton University Press, 1990).

Joubert-Laurencin, Hervé, *Pasolini. Portrait du poète en cinéaste* (Paris: Cahiers du Cinéma, 1995).

Levergeois, Bertrand, *Pasolini. L'alphabet du refus* (Paris: Editions du Félin, 2005).

Mancini, Michele and Giuseppe Perrella, *Pier Paolo Pasolini: corpi e luoghi* (Rome: Theorema, 1981).

Micciché, Lino, *Pasolini nella città del cinema* (Venice: Marsilio, 1999).

Naldini, Nico, *Pasolini, una vita* (Turin: Einaudi, 1989).

Pasolini, special issue of *Revue d'esthétique* 3 (1982).

Pier Paolo Pasolini, special issue of *Cinema & Cinema* 43 (May–August 1985).

Rohdie, Sam, *The Passion of Pier Paolo Pasolini* (London-Bloomington: BFI–Indiana University Press, 1995).

Schwartz, Barth David, *Pasolini Requiem* (New York: Pantheon, 1992).

Siciliano, Enzo, *Pasolini. A Biography*, trans. John Shepley (New York: Random House, 1982).

Siti, Walter and Franco Zabagli (eds), *Pasolini per il cinema*, 2 vols (Milan: Mondadori, 2001).

Snyder, Stephen, *Pier Paolo Pasolini* (Boston: Twayne, 1980).

Stack, Oswald [Jon Halliday] (ed.), *Pasolini on Pasolini* (London: Thames & Hudson, in association with the BFI, 1969).

Viano, Maurizio, *A Certain Realism. Making Use of Pasolini's Film Theory and Practice* (Berkeley, Los Angeles, London: University of California Press, 1993).

Willemen, Paul (ed.), *Pier Paolo Pasolini* (London: BFI, 1977).

Zigaina, Giuseppe, *Pasolini e la morte* (Venice: Marsilio, 1987).

Index

and from Verga nautical metaphors, imaginative representations, an archaic taste for words and the unadorned directness of the speakers. Through this detailed work of bringing together diverse elements, Visconti's mode of expression is pared down to essentials where phrases appear to have been sculpted as necessary and irreplaceable. The simplicity, the bareness of the dialogue is the consequence of progressive purifications, subtractions, transfigurations. The achieved simplicity is not the result of spontaneity, but rather of a fixed epic-sacral rhythm articulated by the archaic sounds of dialect and their characteristic beat. The frequent recourse to repetition, a style used by Verga, aside from being a device for transforming speech into a more popular form, constitutes what might be called a strophic form, like a stanza, imprinted with a musical timbre or an epic-ritual sonority.

In this regard (aside from what has already been systematically observed by other scholars)[8] is the way speech has been structured in certain scenes in the film, such as the return of the fisherman from the sea at its beginning:[9]

> RAIMONDO: Zu' Giuvanni Sigaretta, ni pigghiastivu pisci? (Uncle Giovanni Sigaretta, did you catch any fish?)
> LORENZO: 'A pozzu purtari 'a valanza? (Can I bring you the scales?)
> SIGARETTA: Ni pugghiammu assai. 'A putiti purtari 'a valanza. (We caught a lot. You can bring the scales.)
> NINO: E tu, Angilu Malaterra, ni pigghiasti pisci? (And you, Angelo Malaterra, did you catch any fish?)
> ANGELO: Pocu ni pigghiai, pocu. (Not very many, just a few.)

Or, part of the conversation between 'Ntoni and Cola after the former's return from Catania:

> COLA: Ti voi maritari, 'Ntoni? (Do you want to get married, 'Ntoni?)

8 Lino Micciché, *Visconti e il neorealismo. Ossessione, La terra trema, Bellissima*, Venice: Marsilio, 1990, 123–127.

9 The dialogues in Sicilian that will be cited from now on are taken from the screenplay obtained by Montesanti in 1951. They are reproduced in Enzo Ungari (ed.), *La terra trema*, Bologna: Cappelli, 1977.

'NTONI: Sì, mi uogghiu martiari, Cola! E tu, non ci ll'ài 'na caru-
sidda sutt'occhiu? (What about you, don't you have your eye on
some girl?)
COLA: No, iu, non ci nn'aiu carusi sutt'occhiu. (No, I don't have
my eye on a girl.)
'NTONI: Iu sì, iu ci ll'aiu 'na carusa sutt'occhiu. (I do, I have my
eye on a girl.)

Certain poetic dramatizations of words come to mind, which
also have literary echoes, like the scene in which the mother
embraces her children who had just escaped death, repeating
the word 'figghiu' (son, child) a number of times.

The ritual aspect of the language is also emphasized by
a resort to proverbs, most of them translated directly from
I Malavoglia, and often used to end a sequence, sealing it
with an epigraph. But, above and beyond these pre-established popular formulas, Visconti borrows the generally epic-
aphoristic tone of conversations from the characters who
are speaking, and from Verga, for example, his manner of
using mottos, full of meaning, that is also poetic (COLA: 'U
munnu, nun è bbonu, accussì / The world is not good like
that': 'NTONI: '... 'U mari è siccu e 'a nuttata è nira ...' / The
sea is dry and the night is black ... ', etc.). In this archaic fash-
ioning of language, even single words were carefully chosen.
While there is never a concession to casual and improvised
chit-chat, typical of a certain kind of realism, or of chit-chat
for its own the sake that is somewhat redundant with respect
to the story, each term Visconti uses is always perfectly calibrated for its semantic weight and poetic richness. Words
that might seem obviously modern are not used in *La terra
trema*, lest they would be found out of place in the utterances
of the fishermen from Aci Trezza living in a closed universe
where Visconti suspends time and history to an even greater
degree than they are suspended in reality.

Even the choice of words and pronunciation with which
Visconti tells the story in a Marxist key of exploitation and
growing consciousness is strictly faithful to an ancient, classic repertory. 'Nuàutri semo 'i scecchi di travagghiu!' /'We